Hot Coffee and Cold Truth

HOT COFFEE

and

COLD TRUTH

Living and Writing
the West

Edited by W. C. JAMESON

University of New Mexico Press

Albuquerque

12 11 10 09 08 07 06   1 2 3 4 5 6 7

LIBRARY OF CONGRESS CATALOGING-IN-PUBLICATION DATA

Hot coffee and cold truth : living and writing the West /
    [compiled by] W.C. Jameson.
        p. cm.
Thirteen essays by American writers on how
    living in the West is fundamental to their writing.
        ISBN-13: 978-0-8263-4061-0 (pbk. : alk. paper)
        ISBN-10: 0-8263-4061-X (pbk. : alk. paper)
1. Authors, American—20th century—Biography.
2. West (U.S.)—In literature.
3. Landscape in literature.
4. Setting (Literature)
5. Authorship. I. Jameson, W. C., 1942–
        PS129.H67 2006
        810.9'3278—dc22

                              2006021745

DESIGN AND COMPOSITION: *Mina Yamashita*

Contents

Eye of the Human Storm:
An Introduction

W. C. Jameson

The genesis of this anthology began more than two decades ago in a large bookstore across the street from the University of Texas campus where I encountered *The Time It Never Rained*, a novel by Elmer Kelton, from an extensive selection of fiction related to Texas and the American West.

Back home, wedged into a comfortable recliner with a cup of tea, I read Kelton's stunning story. Captivated after the first few pages of incomparable prose and believable western characters in a memorable western setting, I completed the book in a matter of hours and felt it to be one of the finest literary novels I'd ever read, one which people would still be reading one hundred years from now.

A nonfiction writer with several marginally successful books to my credit, I held serious aspirations to write a masterpiece comparable to Kelton's. However, suffering from a lack of experience as well as a lack of mentoring, I longed to ask Kelton how he did what he did. Where did he come up with the words? How did he know how to coax them onto the page and arrange them with such skillful expertise? I wanted to ask him how the western landscape sparked his imagination, inspired his ideas, and influenced his style. I yearned to know more about him, about his obvious, intimate connection to the land, a relationship that he adroitly manifested between the covers of his books.

Much later I encountered the poetry of Laurie Wagner Buyer and experienced the same kind of desire to know how she wrote the way she did. Crafted from a life of fruitless toiling in the landscapes of the West and of the heart, her lines reached out from the pages to move me to the point where I could feel the wind coming off the mountain, smell the moist earth, hear the whinny of horses in the corral and the honking of geese as they flew south across a cold, overcast sky.

Throughout the years other writers, from vagabond poets to academicians, had the same effect on me. When I had the opportunity, I asked them about their lives and what inspired them to write. I wanted to know how the American West influenced what they wrote. Eager to listen and learn, I reveled in each nugget of knowledge, cherished every insightful jewel that I might use in my own quest to become a better writer.

When speaking at conferences, conducting seminars, or teaching classes, I discovered that participants and students often asked me similar types of questions. The information I passed along was gleaned from the writers I had long admired and tried to emulate. Recognizing that there were others who longed to learn from the masters, I decided to compile a series of essays by writers who felt that living in the West was fundamental to their writing. To quote Wallace Stegner from *On Teaching and Writing Fiction*, "reading the words of these masters, each from the core of heart and knowledge, is to hear the intensely pure and strangely powerful spirit at the eye of the human storm."

There are a number of common denominators among the contributors to this collection that are relative to their ongoing success. The first is a manifest, intense, and memorable connection to the land. Some stated that the western landscape *made* them write, that they were not writers before they came under the spell of this inspirational geography. For many, the West provided experience and, ultimately, inspiration for the settings in their nonfiction, fiction, and poetry. This powerful environment represented such an important influence on these writers that they dedicated themselves to presenting this unusual milieu, whether harsh or gentle, so that others might discover, understand, and appreciate its truest reality.

Secondly, all of them possess a keen curiosity, a probing desire to seek out other people and times, a certain wanderlust to discover what lies beyond the limits of the cities, to see what can be found beyond the next ridge, a need to know new horizons. Each of them, as well, acknowledges that they were stimulated to explore the depths and breadths of literature, to see what others had written, to try and understand how and why previous masters wrote the way they did. Many speak of their introduction to good literature at home, in high school, or in college. There are remarkable similarities in their influences: Shakespeare, George Eliot's *Silas Marner*, Stephen Crane's *The Red Badge of Courage*, Hemingway's *The Old Man and the Sea*, Emily Dickinson's poetry, Mark Twain's fiction. They also speak of their indebtedness to other writers, mentors and teachers, and editors and agents, who blazed the literary trails before them, who both inspired and assisted them in their creative journey.

Lastly, but perhaps most importantly, desire and passion are common components in the makeup of these writers. Many of them took substantial risks, even quitting good jobs, to write. They have endured criticism, even experienced periods of rejection and near poverty, but they never gave up. They believed in themselves, and the writing process, and continued to pursue their dream. They never stopped creating and in doing so they learned that there are no tricks to good writing, no secrets to publication, no easy answers for success. There is just hard work, commitment, persistence, and patience.

Author Win Blevins opens this anthology expressing his affinity for, and kinship with, aspects of the western landscape, physical and cultural, human and wildlife, indigene and immigrant. Blevins maintains these elements bind the writer to the place. Coupled with his passion for place is another for literature and the arts, and more, a craving to write about what goes on in the historic and contemporary places he loves. Blevins speaks of his own wanderlust and curiosity. He is always wondering what is "out there," and he wants to go find it, whatever it is. He longs to walk to the next horizon just to see the color of the country beyond, to "hear that lonesome whistle blow." Blevins moved from the urban jungles of Los Angeles to the Rocky Mountains years ago. He felt a call to write about the amazing country and its special people.

The land, says poet Laurie Wagner Buyer, was her life, her inspiration, her "sassy Muse," her reason for being alive. She confesses the West was her lover, and her love affair with the West was as deep, profound, and sensual as any that could happen between two human beings. Buyer is known for exploring the intimate connections between people, their hearts, and the land in her award-winning poetry.

Margaret Coel opens her essay with an expression of her connections to the "spirits" of the West, the land, and the people. She speaks of how she can "feel" the past, of encountering the ghosts of the Indians and earliest settlers who once lived here. Coel's focus is on the historical West and why the past matters, all of which is intertwined with family stories. An old maxim in writing, Coel says, is "write what you know," but she encourages others to "write what you don't know, because then you will have the pleasure of finding out." Coel's own curiosity, and quest for knowledge, led her to research people and places that eventually became the characters, settings, and plots of her books. She says the discovery, the finding out, was the adventure.

Don Coldsmith is a product of the West in which he lives and writes. He walks the land, explores the landscape, and listens to what the people have to say, particularly the natives. The intimacy he derives from his experiences is translated into his numerous writings. Coldsmith believes in the importance, the necessity, and the joy of reading. Reading, he says, is a prerequisite for all writers, as is curiosity and its role in research and writing.

Robert J. Conley believes in the importance of in-depth research in both fiction and nonfiction. Good writing and good literature are important to communicating history as well as morals, and the best way to learn to become an author, Conley says, is to "read, read, read." Conley insists that writing well is hard work. At the same time, he says, it is fun. Conley developed his writing chops at an early age. At ten he read Shakespeare and others to get the feel for how the masters put together a tale. Today, Conley is considered such a master by his peers.

David Dary offers practical advice relative to the writing of history by cautioning the writer not to be inhibited by a lack of higher education. In fact, Dary, a longtime academician, suggests a writer might be better off without the degrees. Good writing about history, the kind we all like to read, is also good storytelling, he says. It requires fact as well as emotion, two essential ingredients in any good story, whether fiction or nonfiction. Never write dull history, Dary warns.

Max Evans, who came to writing after working as a cowboy, a soldier, prospector, and a painter, believes in the value of reading the classics and learning from the masters, regardless of what genre one wishes to pursue. Evans, who writes with stunning realism, cautions beginning writers about wanting too much too soon and points out that good writing is hard work and that success may not arrive for years.

Bill Gulick delivers priceless insight into the profession of writing as well as the business of publishing. Known for his well-crafted novels and beautifully written nonfiction books, Gulick has seen his work earn important awards and made into films. He also addresses the importance of committed editors and agents and how mentoring can shape the lives of all writers.

Best-selling author Paulette Jiles likens creative writing, especially that associated with crafting the novel, to "going in search of buried treasure." She writes of the all-important quest that is found within stories, yet often mirrors life. Jiles's own quest to explore and research has allowed her to master the territory of the literary novel.

For over two generations, Elmer Kelton, a polite, quiet, and gentle man who is often mobbed at book signings, has been an inspiration to thousands of writers. Kelton has crafted powerful, literary novels set in the West, mostly in his beloved Texas. Western culture and landscape are authentic in Kelton's writings and readers react strongly. Having been raised in a ranching family that lived and worked on the land, the life of the working cowboy was part and parcel of his growing up. It has been said that Kelton's development and presentation of western landscapes take on the importance of a major character in his books.

Robert Utley believes in being in the places he writes about, of walking the trails and the hillsides that were settings for historical events. Utley believes in the importance of thoroughly understanding the geography of a place in order to interpret its history. He hears the sounds of the winter-dried blades of grass under his feet, smells the tang of the mountain or prairie air in his nostrils. Armed with these sensations, as well as his passion for the West and its people, Utley's essays leap from their pages into the consciousness of the reader.

Richard S. Wheeler, a writer who has given so much of his time and energy to helping young, hopeful writers, relates his own efforts to grow into a writer for the ages and not simply for the markets. He speaks of agents and editors who played significant roles in his career. Even more critical, Wheeler discusses chasing the all-important dream, of obstacles encountered along the way, and the disappointments and rewards of writing. ∪

Popeye in a Wide-Brimmed Hat

Win Blevins

Win Blevins
(Photo by Laurie Wagner Buyer)

Win Blevins came out of Missouri and Arkansas and went through a whirlwind of colleges and jobs. At thirty-three, while serving as principal movie and theater critic for the *Los Angeles Herald-Examiner*, he discovered his calling—writing books. Nineteen volumes of fiction, informal history, and lexicography have followed. His historical novel about Crazy Horse, *Stone Song*, won the Spur Award and the Mountains and Plains Booksellers Award. He won another Spur Award for his first novel in the Rendezvous series, *So Wild a Dream*, and was named Writer of the Year in 2003 by Wordcraft Circle of Native Writers and Storytellers for his *Dictionary of the American West*.

A devoted westerner, hiker, river-rafter, and mountaineer, Blevins lives and writes in a remote corner of the canyonlands of Utah.

You ask me to talk about what I love? Westerners and the West?

Love isn't easy to explain, and it's dangerous to talk about it.

Westerners are like the land. We roar like big rapids, pounding past big boulders. We're hard and dry and unyielding, like the barren, cinnamon-colored mountains of the Mojave Desert. We are as colorful as the exuberant wildflowers of a mountain meadow, and silky as the elegant mahogany skin of a manzanita tree.

Maybe we westerners are like the land because we live hard up next to it. We don't shape it—it molds us. The personalities, the character profiles of other Americans, maybe, are produced by the influence of church, town, newspapers, television, and so on. Westerners are sculpted, for good and ill, by harder hands.

We also grow where there is more room. We build our homes farther apart. When we talk, we stand back a little. We even park our cars on the street with more space between the bumpers. We walk, ride, and drive most days across distances populated only by ravens, grasses, cacti, rock ridges, and a sky empty of all but blinding blue. Our minds are neither busy nor populous.

We are no cookie-cutter people, nor manufactured on any assembly line. Having room to grow as we choose, we craft ourselves into forms that are no doubt damned odd. Some of us develop rambunctious spirits and independent minds. Some of us become queer and perverse. Most of us, either way, are distinctly whatever we choose to be. Our personalities are lava rock, not whipped cream. When you talk to a real westerner, you never know what you'll discover next, because he or she is an original.

I find this true, partly, even in our cities. Westerners whose landscape, sadly, is pavement and skyscrapers, who see wildlife manufactured by Ford or Toyota, still have a core of this Popeye spirit—I am what I am, deal with it. Maybe, over enough decades, our city cousins are losing what's left of this attitude, and they'll be poorer for it.

The canyonlands are the particular piece of the West where Meredith and I choose to live, where we built our home. I first came here three decades ago, driving up from Los Angeles to run a river. I came for a week, stayed a month, then came back, and back, and back.

Our bedroom has a picture window facing up Cottonwood Wash. Thirty or forty miles to the north, the Abajo Mountains make the edge of our sky jagged. The peaks rise thousands of feet above the red desert floor, far above the humming doings of humans. Most mornings the sun wakes us up, and we watch the bluffs on the west side of the wash turn from brown-gray to red-gold. The glow makes my heart ping.

Between our home and the Abajos await more sites of rock art and ruins than we will ever be able to hike to. There's an astro-archaeological site, a place where the ancients used great stones to mark the winter and summer solstices, which I feel drawn to. I want to go there soon and see autumn turn to winter, spring pivot into summer.

I've also hiked those mountains. Running east and west along them is the highway that leads to Lake Powell, a marvelous playground, and unfortunately the graveyard of Glen Canyon, may it never be forgotten. Beside that road is Natural Bridges National Monument, where I love to duck down into the canyon and walk below the bridges, and look up in awe. On the other side of the highway is Grand Gulch, an enormous maze of canyons that leads to the San Juan River, a thousand-thousand secrets to explore.

The San Juan is what first brought me here. It heads up in the mountains of Colorado, snowmelt trickling in rivulets to make swift creeks and then knit into a boisterous river. It parades out onto the desert, survives imprisonment at Navajo Dam, and then swings our way. From our little town it rages some eighty or so miles to Lake Powell. I have floated it many times, and I yearn to go back.

To ride that river in a raft, to course through its deep canyons and geologic marvels, is to experience the life of the Earth of tens of millions of years ago, and feel something of the enduring life of this wondrous planet. In the end, let us go to the river, and listen to its melodies.

I wish everyone knew what this country has to teach. It is not a wisdom of the head, but of the heart. In my books, I strive to Ziploc some if it for Americans and others elsewhere. Dwellers in big cities particularly need it. But words cannot carry, in full, the rhythms of the rocks.

Let me remind you of what my country looks like. You've seen it in a score or more of John Ford westerns. You've been assaulted by it in a hundred television commercials for pick-up trucks and four-wheel drive vehicles. And you've seen it in the movie *Thelma and Louise.* There at the end, when Geena Davis and Susan Sarandon drive their car off the cliff—that's *my* country. That precipice of red sandstone is almost visible from our windows. If you give it more attention than a helicopter shot, it will bring solace to your soul.

Yes, the people hold me here as much as the land.

Men and women in the West possess first-hand minds. In a book-store in a college town in northern Idaho thirty years ago, I saw a giant of a man stride in wearing a big hat and a sheepskin coat. I asked the store owner who he was.

"One of our Basque sheepherders," he said. "He's been out for the winter and this is probably his first trip into town."

"What does he want?" I asked. My thought, I'm ashamed to admit, was: What does a fellow such as this want in a bookstore? Maybe *Penthouse*?

The owner just said, "Watch what he buys."

After a while, the Basque-American brought to the cash register the complete works of the Russian anarchist-philosopher Mikhail Bakunin. A lesson learned.

Consider just one realm where westerners do not, intellectually, walk the tracks laid down for us—environmental issues, which are big in my heart. When I talk with city people about them, especially easterners, I hear recycled versions of the lines I've read in the *Washington Post, Los Angeles Times,* and *USA Today,* or at best press releases from the Sierra Club. When I speak with westerners, especially old-timers, about the challenges to our environment, I often find modulation and reason. Often I hear something I don't know. Westerners seem to be less doctrinaire, less sloganeering, less combative, and more thoughtful about the long-term impact on our water, soil, and air. That's not just because they have a love for the land and a wisdom about it that outsiders can't approach. It is because they think for themselves.

Twice I have been called by pollsters like those of the Gallup outfit. They give me a set of answers to choose from, but the choices are citified. I can't choose any because none fit. It is like trying to fit a silk slipper on an eagle claw.

Westerners are original until it hurts. Several decades ago, Cottonwood Wash was inundated with its once-in-fifty-years flood. The highway and its businesses got swamped. The woman who ran the local trading post had a flock of chickens. Several drowned, others nearly did. She saved many of them, so she claims, by applying mouth-to-beak resuscitation.

This same woman, according to report, let her fingernails grow one summer until they curved under, like claws. She cut them, strung them, and sold them to a tourist as a bear-claw necklace.

There are wilder doings of this woman I could tell, by common consent entirely true, but the statute of limitations hasn't run out on her deeds, and I like living.

It's hard to exaggerate about western lands. More than a century ago Jim Bridger, the mountain man, dropped in on a Bozeman newspaper editor to tell him about Yellowstone Park. After a couple of geyser stories, the newsman threw him out. He wasn't going to be taken in by old Jim's lies. This is a country bigger than any lie you can tell about it.

I lived in the Yellowstone country, on three sides of the park, for two decades. It is another piece of western divinity I've been privileged to know well and to love, and part of what I love is the animals.

I love the osprey. They build their nests on the tops of the telephone poles when the poles are near the river. From there, they catch, with atavistic fierceness, the river's trout. A fly fisherman can be a pleasure to watch. To watch an osprey hunt is a primal thrill.

I love bald eagles. One summer I guided tourists on a ten-mile float down the Snake River in Grand Teton National Park. For me the highlight in May and June was watching fledglings in a certain eagle's nest. They started as hungry beaks thrusting greedily up toward an airborne parent. A few weeks later they were fragile chicks falling out of their nest and wooshing along on invisible air currents. In the end, they learned to soar.

When I go to native ceremonies, I wear an eagle claw around my neck. Not a single curved point, but the whole foot, big and sharp. For me it has power, and power makes people nervous.

I love golden eagles. I have found their nests in the crags. I have collected their feathers. One afternoon, Meredith and I watched two ravens wage hit-and-run warfare on a golden eagle, probably trying to keep him away from their nest. The ravens won.

I love ravens, too. One of my novels is called *Raven Shadow*. Some day I might write more about them, so I'll save my raven thoughts for those pages, for another time.

I love the moose, ugly in a way that can only be described as comically beautiful. Veteran westerners consider the moose more dangerous than the grizzly bear.

I love the wolf. One night, on the south edge of Yellowstone Park, I lay in my sleeping bag and listened to wolves howling. How far away, I had no idea. When I returned to so-called civilization, the weekly newspaper informed me that a wolf had been shot and killed that very day about five miles from where I had slept.

When the wolf was reintroduced to Yellowstone Park, I made the pilgrimage with many other gawkers to their favorite valley and watched them. They are not rapacious predators, as we have been taught to think.

We can learn from them. We should learn from them. In native myth, they are brothers to the raven.

I love the grizzly bear. All through the 1990s, I did a vision quest each autumn in Yellowstone. Every time, the rangers got me to sign an affidavit that testified that I knew what I was walking into, understood that piece of country was a high-danger grizzly area.

I was avid to go. Sure, I saw bear sign, sometimes saw scat right in my campground. Once I saw a bear. The most memorable time, though, was the trip when I brought my son Adam along and a griz joined us uninvited.

That night I crept into the tent. Though it was my custom to sleep outside, I was chattering with cold. Inside I lit a couple of candles to raise the temperature a degree or two and stretched out nude in my sleeping bag. About fifty yards away in the sagebrush, my son Adam was sleeping.

I heard the griz nosing around. I wasn't worried about her (let's suppose this was a she-bear). If she wanted to eat me, I would have already been turned into gastric juices. But, oh my God, Adam! The father in me quaked. I jumped up and ran out of the tent stark naked and around to the back. "Adam," I yelled. "Adam, are you all right?" This call was a violation of our mutual pledge to conduct the vision quest in complete silence.

"I'm fine, Dad. Go back to sleep."

I did, or at least I ensconced myself within that orange nylon, aglow with candlelight, and closed my eyes and tried.

When we got back to the car a day and a half later, and speech was permitted, I apologized to Adam for disturbing his quest.

"That's okay, Dad. But who was that standing behind you?"

It took me a minute to realize what he saw. That griz must have thought I was one crazy white man.

And then there are the landforms. For me, the shapes of the Earth are poetry. Their phrases are riverbanks, hills, mountain ranges, and their rhymes are decades, centuries, millennia, eons.

I want to spend days walking out across the land, or driving through it (not as good—too fast), or flying over it in a small plane (for another angle), or boating through it, and experiencing again the landforms. I want to soak my eyes in the way a mountain ridge juts up sharp and steep against an outrageous blue sky, then I want to feel that rhythm in my legs, mounting with it. I want to see again how slickrock undulates, smooth and sexy as a woman's belly, and feel its curve in my body and my balance, how sandstone spires stand like sentinels and their shadows tick-tock across the sagebrush.

I want to boat the San Juan again, or swim it in my life jacket, and experience truly the way a river makes her moves, how she re-sculpts a sand bank, tumbles over a rock shelf, roars through a fall of rocks as big as sheds.

Then, relaxing in an eddy, I can look up at the canyon walls soaring a couple thousand feet above my head and see how this very river made similar moves ten thousand years ago, and a hundred thousand, and a million, and ten million. She carved a lacy terrace here, where now some grasses and a few cedars perch. There, she hammered a passage right through a wall of stone. Mostly, though, she sculpted sheer, mighty walls, vertical cliffs, simple and declarative. They don't speak words, the language of the mind. They sing the patterns of time.

Landforms.

Did I say something about being a crazy white man? Be not deceived. Like many other westerners, I am not exactly white. I'm a jumble, descended from Cherokees who walked the Trail of Tears, Irish farmers, and Welshmen, all westering Americans.

This brings me to the subject of Indians. I like Indian people.

Here, along the San Juan River, I live among the Navajo. Every day I see them and on most days hear Navajo spoken. Many Navajos are friends. This county is mostly red. One Ute reservation is twelve miles north of town, another is an hour's drive to the east. A little to the south are the Hopi. Within three or four hours' drive are the Pueblo people of central New Mexico. In the Yellowstone country, I lived around Crows, Sioux, Shoshones, Blackfeet, and others, and came to know some of them well.

We are creeping up to a matter that is private. I do not propose to talk much about my spirituality, but I will say this: I am a carrier of the sacred pipe and I walk its red road. I am a pourer of the sweat lodges, a veteran of the sun dance and of the vision quest. That is enough to make public.

But back to Indian people. I love their resilience. They walk a hard road and often do it with a quirky humor that is indescribably their own. Traditional Indians have wisdom we can learn from, as they can learn from the way we understand the world. I have learned from them and seek to teach them what I know.

At the same time, Indians often betray their wisdom. They wreck their lives, and their children's. Alcohol, unemployment, lack of education, disease—their afflictions know no end. I celebrate Indian people and I grieve for them. Among other westerners of my circle, they bind me to this place.

It is time for me to bang another door open. We westerners get stereotyped as Marlboro Men. We wear that sort of hat and boot, we ride, we hunt, we fish, belong to the National Rifle Association, and we chew tobacco. You know the clichés.

The last thing a true westerner would ever be is a stereotype. Don't I wear the hat and boots?

I used to.

Don't I hunt?

Yes, and have brought the meat home.

Have I fished the swift mountain rivers?

Yes, and brought trout to the net.

Have I gone deep into country most people never see, and loved being far from the nearest telephone?

Absolutely. In fact, I did much more. I put on the climber's harness and tied the rope to it and my partner and I mounted great peaks, completed difficult ascents, accomplished first ascents. For a decade climbing was my passion.

Did I ride horses?

I did, and owned them, cared for them, and traveled the land on their backs trailing cattle down the mountain to winter pasture.

Did I run cattle? No, but I branded them, smelled their burning hides, dined on their oysters. But no more.

My point is that all of that is irrelevant. Whatever of those very western activities I participated in, they were not the home of my heart. My home, my passion, always, was literature and music. I read. I wrote. I played. I went to concerts. Westerners are not what you expect.

First the music. If you entered my study on most days, you would find me writing about the deserts and mountains and plains. But I wouldn't be listening, as I wrote, to Waylon Jennings or the masterful Willie Nelson. My earphones would be full of Beethoven, Mahler, Brahms, Bach, Mozart.

As a kid in St. Louis I loved two things: playing baseball and playing the piano. As a young man, not having been drafted by the St. Louis Cardinals, I played in bands and orchestras and wind ensembles, every imaginable group at every opportunity. I wanted two careers, two paths, two paths to ecstasy—reading and writing, playing and listening. I couldn't imagine one without the other, and I still struggle with that.

I tried to combine my passions. I went to graduate school at Columbia University in New York and spent as much time in Carnegie

Hall as I did in the classroom. At another university, I quit a doctoral program because my advisor wanted me to stop playing music and hurl myself entirely into books.

Finally, I thought I hit on the solution: I would spend my life writing about music.

The Rockefeller Foundation supported my fantasy. The *Los Angeles Times* got me started as a music and theater reviewer. The *Los Angeles Herald-Examiner* made me the principal classical music critic, then drama critic, then movie critic and entertainment editor. I was in heaven.

Except that it felt wrong.

After five years, I figured out what was bothering me. I was spending my life writing about what artists did, in music, in theater, in film. But I was only commenting while they were doing. I felt like the high school boy who leans against the gym wall during a dance making flip remarks about what clumsy dancers his friends were. It struck me, forcibly, that that fellow doesn't get to touch the girls, but his waltzing friends do.

I wanted to make art, not comment on it. When I got a shot at a book contract, I leapt at the road of full-time writing. It was the right choice. My best instrument is the written word.

I will not tell here the story of the many books, screenplays, and articles that have poured from the fountainhead of that choice. If you want that story, read my books. When you do, read them deeply and truly and you will know me better than any human being does, except for my family.

OK, OK, I hear you grumbling. If I am really a devotee of classical music, if I write about music and theater and movies, then in what way am I a westerner? And in what way a western writer?

I told you. We westerners don't ride the rails you lay down for us, but go our own way. Let me tell you how it works in my case.

My mom and dad were both born in Arkansas of farming families in podunk towns. The towns had this in common: If you spit at either one from a moving train, you would miss.

My parents came to Earth from the loins of people who gravitated west looking for a better life. By the time they were born, one family had risen to scratching out a subsistence on red dirt acreage they actually owned. The other had moved to town and lived on odd jobs.

I was the first of either family to attend high school. There, I got an introduction, sort of, to the literary heritage of the English language in the form of *Macbeth, Julius Caesar, Silas Marner, The Red Badge of Courage,* the poems of Emily Dickinson. All of these, I recall, were taught in my high school. They made less impression, I believe, than the stories I heard at home, and they shaped me even less.

At home I heard Bible stories, naturally, full of righteousness, dangers, occasional miracles, and an ever-angry God. I heard stories of hunting and fishing. My grandpa sent my dad and his brother out hunting with a .22 rifle and one cartridge. They were to bring back meat for the pot without wasting ammunition. I heard stories about marvels and monsters in those dark, mysterious woods, which sounded like wonderlands to me.

It was my mom, though, who summarized for me, long after my father's death, what I got out of those stories. According to her, my dad, as a child, used to sit on the porch of the farmhouse on summer evenings and winter nights and wait for the train. The rails of the Missouri-Pacific railroad ran from St. Louis, passed through Little Rock, nipped the edge of my family's farm, and headed for Texarkana and points beyond. These were unknown, unimaginable, enticing places my dad couldn't even name. He sat on that porch and waited to hear the whistle. When the train crossed the Hot Springs highway just west of our farm, the engineer tooted a warning to drivers.

Dad listened to that lonely whistle sounding in the night and made himself a promise. One day, when he grew up, when he could follow his heart's desire, he would go wherever that train went. In my mom's story I discovered, for the first time, how I am my father's son.

My father kept his promise. His first job, at seventeen, was working for the railroad. He rode the rails on a motorcar and repaired signals. When my brother and I were small, we lived in little towns along the tracks, south from St. Louis toward Texas and west toward the Rocky Mountains. We lived in Colorado one summer because of his job, a job he kept for forty-eight years.

Going to see the elephant, the forty-niners heading west on the California Trail called it. Walking to the next horizon to see what color of country lies beyond. To be a westerner is to hear that lonesome whistle blow, wonder what waits out there, and then go find out.

As a writer I am what I am. Deal with it.

The traditional characters of the western are cowboys, settlers, soldiers, sodbusters, and the like. They are seen as people who conquered a rough land, killed off the wild animals, and bent the great West to their will.

But what was their will? To run cattle, build railroads, establish towns with churches and schools. To wipe out the wilderness and bring civilization. Or so goes the myth.

My own favorite historical characters, the ones I like to write about, are mountain men and Indians. They love the land as it is. They live on the great buffalo herds who feed on the grass the settlers' cattle will want. What the settlers called wilderness my Indians called home. The wilderness the settlers want to tame, that's the spirit my mountain men live for.

In the stereotypical version of the myth of the West, we're told, white people conquered the Indians, tamed the wild land and wild animals, and replaced all with the glories of civilization.

I do not care to read the action-adventure novels that paint this silly picture. How We Won the West, with scenes of cheap sentiment.

Warped history, and fake theatricality, starring cowboys as knights of the plains who ride white steeds, all set to the marching band music of John Philip Sousa. I do not regard white settlement as a noble conquest, but as a tale equally of triumph and tragedy for red man and white.

So I tell other kinds of stories, of those people who loved the West before cows and cowboys, who took their mountains and deserts with a sauce of danger. I celebrate wildness and how it nurtures the human spirit. I agree with Gus in *Lonesome Dove* when he asked Call, "Did it ever occur to you that when we came up here and shot up the Indians and the Mexicans, we killed off everything that was interesting in this country?"

With other writers, I'd like to create a new myth of the West, one with the grandeur of the stories of the Greek gods. We could recount the times of great heroes of one kind, the red men, being supplanted by a new pantheon, the white men. These god-like figures would act out the most splendid and unforgettable tale of all, the powers of one great era of human history making way for another. For the old gods were not, in truth, defeated by their enemies but rather pushed off the stage by the relentless force called time, which forever dances the old out of existence, and dances in the new. This is a myth worthy of the West's actual history, and preferable, by far, to the phony patriotic jingle about how the good guys conquered.

Remember, time's next victim will be our own civilization.

People ask me sometimes, what is my creative process like?

Hard to talk about, in my opinion. When you start analyzing creativity, it may go hide in a corner. But the good news is, it will pop up again tomorrow, rambunctious and eager to play, because creativity is natural. It runs and jumps and hollers. What is unnatural, but common, is to suppress it. If you distrust it, or strap it down with rules, or lecture it often enough, it sulks.

My wife Meredith and I have a brainstorming process that works for us. We go to the local café, the only one in town, eat lunch, and play "What If?" with the characters we are writing about. What if Mike's hobby is riding motorcycles? What if Lisa tattles on Joanne? What if Tom walks in the room at the very moment?

When it's working, we don't slow down long enough to analyze the answers. We toss the ball of imagination higher and higher. When we find something we love, we whoop. Then, we take the ideas we love most back to the keyboard. This process works for us. Remember, creativity is play.

People also ask me about my preceptors as a writer. Who held up the lantern to show me the way? Surprisingly, it is not a tale of the plains, deserts, and mountains of the West, but of the sea.

At nineteen years of age, attending a Bible college, I was an imposter. In my mind I had thrown over all those fundamentalist ideas, had overturned the throne and banished the silly Jehovah. Never, before or since, have I felt so lonely.

My hidden sanctuary was reading. In books I discovered worlds beyond the philosophy of fundamentalists, worlds I believed existed but had never seen. By coincidence, my eureka was Hemingway's *The Old Man and the Sea*.

In a sense, I had not read good novels until then. Oh, I'd turned the pages, but I was studying, not reading. I was trying to figure out what society thought about the books, what the teachers wanted me to learn about them.

The first book I approached as an authentic reader, seeking personal illumination, was Hemingway's short novel. It picked me up, shook me, lifted me to the heights, plunged me to the depths, left me wrung out, and on the last page left me gasping for breath.

I haven't read it in forty-seven years, but now I take the risk of describing what I remember. It is the tale of an old man, a Cuban, who dares to go on an adventure, to risk his life upon the waters and seek their bounty. He catches a great fish. This fish can be his salvation, perhaps his food for the winter. He lashes it to his frail fishing craft. As he makes his way back to the shore where his home stands, sharks attack the big fish. He battles them. Slowly, morsel by morsel, they devour the fish. He arrives at the port with nothing but a skeleton. Defeated, still impoverished, he walks up the hill toward his house, bearing his mast like a cross. Yet, he has garnered a victory of the spirit. He has sought, he has risked, and he has conducted himself honorably, courageously. I found him magnificent.

I read the book in a single sitting, a swoop of exhilaration. Never had I seen such a man, such a world. I was transported. Half a century later, I look back with fondness on the young man who had that experience. And I think among other things, what a very western story it is.

I could recast this primal tale as the story of an Indian, a young Indian, seeking a great blessing, perhaps the hide of a white buffalo. He fails in the physical realm, succeeds in the spiritual. In its essence, its truth, the story would not change one whit.

At the University of Missouri, I was lucky enough to have a teacher who had a huge impact on me, John G. Neihardt. At the time I didn't read his great verse epic *Cycle of the West* or even his seminal *Black Elk Speaks*. The effect of those books, powerful and unforgettable, came later. As a senior I took a course in the writing of poetry from Neihardt, and he taught me the craft and discipline of shaping words into something worthy, and the devotion of love that the writer must bring to the task.

He also taught me something more than that, even today, I cannot easily name. He had a largeness of spirit that is, in my experience, without parallel. He loved and respected human beings, all of them, even lowly undergraduates. He loved and respected the Earth. He hoped, he dreamed, he imagined. Perhaps he was not a great writer, but to me, he was a great man, and I still seek to emulate his largeness of spirit.

Another important influence was the poet, E. E. Cummings. In his vibrant individualism, his love of nature, and his mad originality, even this quintessential New Englander was very like a westerner.

A huge influence was Walt Whitman. *Leaves of Grass* seems to me the first wholly original book America produced. Its view of human nature is new, and utterly American. Its poetic method, still misunderstood and unappreciated, is new and thoroughly American. Even today when I read it, I experience something essential: I *feel* myself and my countrymen and our way of seeing the world, and I see how we are different from the people of the Old World and their old ways. In those pages I know what it is genuinely to be an American, a citizen of the New World.

Onward. The most inspirational and influential writer on me, and I think on all American writing, is the man who grew up in Hannibal, Missouri, where I went to college a hundred miles north of St. Louis, where I spent my childhood. I speak of Mark Twain, in particular, of his two great books, *Life on the Mississippi* and *The Adventures of Huckleberry Finn.*

Most Americans read Huck's story as I did, as kids, or had it read to them. Those who are lucky return to it as adults and find another kingdom of experience and thought. The classic journey, setting out on a raft through an idyllic America, looking for . . . well, that's what you must discover. It has everything: A friend to share the joys and hardships; the nine-hundred-pound gorilla in the corner, slavery; rogues along the way, and decent folks; crazy, wonderful incidents; a sense that life is a nifty adventure, but there are serious things to attend to. At the end of this great journey, Huck comes back to Aunt Polly and the life of convention that he fled. He has to make a choice—the old way or the new. A known, conventional life? Or an authentic life, somewhere else, somewhere unknown?

Huck's choice is expressed in a phrase as eloquent as any in western literature. Feeling boxed in by Aunt Sally's civilization, he supposes he'll "light out for the Territory ahead of the rest."

It's what we westerners do.

My friend, the late Ed Abbey, who was the prose poet of this landscape, used to say he wanted to come back as a buzzard, ride the thermals all day, and at night hang out in the cottonwoods with his friends.

Myself, I'd like to come back as a coyote and yip at the full moon, and the new moon, and the blasting sun, and the fertile rain. I want to sing a song that suggests how grand, eternal, and awesome this planet is, and how quirky, mysterious, comical, and heart-touching are the people who live on it. As a coyote, I can make the music I wish I'd made in this incarnation.

In the meantime, I have stories to write. I live with the characters of imagination, forged from my sense of the historical West and from my experience of the West right now. When enough gather together, like a pack of coyotes, not a herd of cattle, I'll trot along with them and set down the words that tell where they go and what they do and how much fun they have.

I offer you an invitation. Pick up a book and come along. ☋

Red Fox, Wilderness, and the West

Laurie Wagner Buyer

When she is not backpacking in the high country or on the road performing, speaking, and presenting workshops, poet and author Laurie Wagner Buyer lives in Woodland Park, Colorado, where she devotes time to her mentoring and editing business.

Born in Edinburgh, Scotland, Buyer arrived in the American West in 1975. After graduating with highest honors from Montana State University, she worked on ranches across the western states and held jobs as a geological research assistant, business manager for a theater group, assistant librarian, and manager for a fly-fishing resort.

Laurie Wagner Buyer
(Photo by W. C. Jameson)

Buyer's award-winning poetry books include *Red Colt Canyon* and *Glass-Eyed Paint in the Rain*. Her memoir, *Spring's Edge*, won the Beryl Markham Award for Creative Nonfiction from Story Line Press. *Side Canyons*, a novel based on a true story, was published by Five Star Press. The recipient of a Literature Artist Fellowship and numerous grants from the Colorado Council on the Arts, Buyer has worked with the Young Audiences Program and the On-Line Poetry Project.

With an MFA in creative writing from Goddard College in Vermont, and having been featured in *Reader's Digest, The Rocky Mountain News,* and *Persimmon Hill,* Buyer is in demand at conferences and venues across the country.

A red fox three-legs her way over the last inches of asphalt, tips into the ditch, disappears, reappears still gimpy, and limps to the edge of the backyard aspens. Tongue lolling, she turns to stare at my Jeep stopped in the middle of the street. Her paw-raised stance states she is confused and in pain, but her eyes still say *I'm not afraid.* Like her, I do not belong in the Rolling Park subdivision in the mountain town of Woodland Park. Like her, I am confused and in pain. But unlike her I am afraid, more afraid, perhaps, than I've been since I first turned my nose West thirty years ago and followed the scent of wild places to their source.

Though I spotted their tracks often enough in Montana, Wyoming, and Colorado snow to know that fox shared the same space I knew and loved, in a trio of decades I caught only a few glimpses of the actual flesh and blood creatures zipping across the remote roadways. Now, within a handful of weeks, looking out the picture window of my mother's long, low, ranch-style home, I've seen fox a dozen times, sauntering through the trees, trotting up the driveway, sprinting ahead of neighborhood dogs panting in pursuit. Whether my sightings have been of the hurt-paw fox (which I want to assume, but don't know for certain, is female) or of several different foxes, I cannot tell. I like to think, though, that it is the same fox, one who has come down from wilderness haunts to serve as a spirit guide, a divine presence sent to help me find my way through the unsettling ache of being a town dweller for the first time in my adult life.

I hear a car approaching from behind and glance in my rearview mirror. A herd of T-shirted teenagers crammed into a battered, belly-dragging, souped-up Firebird fling their arms in my direction. It looks like the vehicle is trying to take flight. Taking my foot off the Jeep's brake,

I slide to the side of the street as the Firebird flies past, gears growling out a young man's disenchantment with a middle-aged woman who had the audacity to stop and study a crippled fox. I search the trees and find her still there in the shade swiping her injured limb in the air like she's waving. An expression akin to a smirk crosses her face, then she yawns. She's laughing at me, bored beyond belief at my insecure attitude.

Most often, I don't quite comprehend this new uncertainty, still cannot figure out how I ended up here surrounded by houses where, reduced to the fate of walking concrete sidewalks or macadam trails amid traffic, joggers, bicyclists, I feel lost and alone. Yes, stately ponderosa pines grace every spot not covered by buildings and by-ways. Yes, miles and miles of national forest radiate out from the deeded land and I'm allowed to hike there if I hop in the Jeep, drive a few miles to the trail head, pay a fee, and take care where I stop to pee.

Perverse as it sounds, I am spoiled and selfish. At heart I am unwilling to share private landscapes with others. Traversing the same trail as someone else feels adulterous, a sensation ripe with trespass and the sin of my feet kissing soil and rock that I do not know intimately and to which I have no claim. For many years, tucked away in wilderness strongholds or sequestered on remote ranches, I stepped out cabin doors and embraced thousands of acres of untrampled country. I consorted with deer, elk, and moose, paid homage to hawks and ravens, waited for the owl or kildeer's call, stumbled onto fresh bear scat, searched for trout shadows in the streams, allowed the wind to have her wicked way with me, and honored winter's harsh cold and deep snow because the wrathful weather drove the smattering of tourists and summer-season visitors out of the high country. I paid the price for my nefarious love affair with the land through hard work, tending to household chores, and the care and feeding of domestic animals belonging to the men who allowed me to live with them. Never easy, the romantic, passionate highs naturally dipped down into depressed squabbles, cabin-fever complaints, and furious accusations of one-sided affection. Threats meant nothing. The land, the most unyielding of all lovers, simply said, "If you don't like it here, leave."

> The land was never mine for all my wanting
> I came, desired, took
> I never asked. . . .
> Undiscovered now, as ever, she waits.

Until recently, I stayed. I stuck with it because I felt the land's cry, her call for compassion and understanding, for acceptance in a world where people were unable or unwilling to discover her depths. I stayed. Sometimes hanging on with fingernails-gouged-in-the-cliff-edge tenacity. Sometimes against my own better judgment. Sometimes against the concerned advice of family and friends. Sometimes in the face of ridiculous odds and unsavory outcomes. But, I stayed because the land was my life, my inspiration, my sassy Muse, and my reason for being alive. Without the land, without the West, who would I be? Where would I call home?

After my first three years of toughing out a homestead lifestyle on the North Fork of the Flathead River in far northern Montana, I knew I belonged to the West, and the West, in her own intractable, implacable way, belonged to me. It was never a marriage made in heaven. It was always a love affair that hung in delicate balance just above the hellish flames of unhealthy obsession. And, in those matters of the heart, wherein affection and addiction braid need and want inexplicably together, I often found myself an unwitting bystander, a victim of my body's desire for raw earth beneath my feet and my spirit's restless yearning for unmarred horizons and unfettered wandering. I said once that I came West because I fell in love with a man, but I stayed because I fell in love with the land—a true statement when I was twenty, truer still as I stare the shifty gaze of fifty down to the wire. Only now, like the red fox that was hit by a vehicle, attacked by dogs, or caught in a trap,

I'm limping my hesitant way into an uncertain future.

> . . . and the world went to its knees
> before my enraptured face
> and my trembling hand reached out
> to touch the harsh bark of a bare
> aspen tree, steadying myself,
> my legs weak with longing
> and love of the very air.

I endured earlier short separations from the land with braced back and painted-on smiles, but divorce from the land, banishment from a way of life I hold much too dear, is unbearable. The experience remains a kind of pain I struggle to name or give voice to. Agony sounds affected. Grief seems almost superficial. Indescribable loss borders on illusion. After all, how can I lose something that never belonged to me in the first place? Or, why did I allow myself to love something so exquisitely tangible but in the end inaccessible. Once, when my husband's property was being sold, I heard a lifelong neighboring rancher tell him, "It's plumb foolishness to love something that cannot love you back."

> I hesitated only a moment,
> then closed my eyes and sank
> to the wet waiting ground
> where last year's leaves clung
> to me like kisses, sun dogs
> danced on my inner lids
> and I opened myself
> to the seduction of a snipe's
> wind-rushed-in-wings song.

My improbable infatuation with wilderness landscapes caught me unaware. A child who had never camped out, a teenager who had never hiked, a college student who had never seen any animal beyond squirrels and birds in the wild, I harbored no notion whatsoever that the trillion-and-one diamond chips of sunlight reflecting off pristine snow my second morning in Montana would create an engagement more valuable, more binding, than any carat-sized hunk of glass purchased at great price from Zales or Tiffany's. I only knew that once I touched the weathered texture of wind-worn wood and water-smoothed stone, let my lips sip the icy elixir of the river, allowed my unclothed flesh to absorb the caress of spring sun, the sharp nip of autumn's tempestuous breeze, the teasing twist of summer grass around my calves, that I was lost, so in love with the sacredness of dirt and air, all flourishing things, and abundant animal life, that I promised myself that I would do anything to not have to return to the secular world of day jobs, retirement worries, and stressed out nights in front of the television.

> In comparison to the earth's symphony
> our human voices hold
> no magic, no music, no power
> in the remarkable mystery of morning
>
> Worshipping, silenced by other sounds,
> I listen, learning again the solemn
> secrets that recreate the day beyond
> the distant heathen cities.

Like most young women enmeshed in the first great loves of their lives, I began to write when I came West. With no camera, no talent for painting or drawing, the only means I found available to capture the face and complexion of my lover was through words. I wrote small thumbnail sketches at first, like these lines written my first spring in the West:

Raw winds blow in the dawn.
Snow gathers deep
beneath frozen peaks
where the mare stands on guard
her steamy breath enfolding
the one born too soon for spring.

Then, I wrote longer poems and stories, most of which I mailed back to Illinois to my mother and father, sisters, or left-behind friends. After wood and water chores, milking, feeding, cooking, cleaning, whenever I had the free time, if my eyes weren't focused inside the pages of a book, they were glued to yellow legal pads where I scribbled, scratching out a plethora of lines and phrases attempting to find the right words to express the tangle of new-found emotions attached to events that happened daily right outside the door: the river at flood stage, cow elk barking from the opposite bank, coyotes calling, the bewitching cry of the loon, the whoosh of a redtail's wings as it made a dive for chickens scratching scattered seed in the sun, the live-in skunk's rapacious odor, slick birth fluids, nursing the ones that lived, flinging the ones who died on rooftops for ravens, cats mewing for morning milk, spotting a cougar racing from cliff-edge shadow to jack pine sanctuary. I never found enough time, or the proper process to encapsulate everything that bombarded my heart and mind, but I undertook the challenge.

The land holds me . . .
grasps my city-born heart. . . .
Only a log ruin
forsaken walls and windows
seem familiar
but even then,
by cracked reflection I see,
the land holds me.

In an attempt to understand this unwieldy and intractable passion for a barely known landscape, I turned to the men and women who had dedicated their lives and sacrificed their hearts in similar affairs. My first nonfiction article, "A Man Alone," a personality profile on the man I lived with on the North Fork, sold to *Western Horseman* in 1978. The acceptance letter from publisher Dick Spencer and the accompanying check for one hundred dollars set my course. While I received countless rejections for my poetry over the next quarter of a century, my nonfiction writing honoring men and women of the West appeared in magazines like *Farm and Ranch Living, Beef, Horse and Rider, The Fence Post, Cowboy, Roundup,* and *Colorado Central.* The avocation fed my need to work with words and filled my pathetic bank account with just enough funds to purchase postage stamps. I never thought of myself as a writer, or, forbid the sacrilege of even mentioning the holy title, poet. I was merely a backwoods woman, a ranch wife, who loved to linger over language and mess around with metaphors.

I want the rounded wealth of words
language untangled from a poet's tongue
the metric rhyme from which it sprung
the flying past like a flock of birds
I need the magic mystery of words.

When I received mail, people invariably sent similar remarks: You tell it like it is. You say what I wish I could say. Your appreciation of life on the land and your affection for animals shines through. You know what I've been through. Thank you for sharing your stories.

What readers responded to, pure and simple, was the bittersweet romance of it all. They, too, were engaged in their own pitfall-ridden, sometimes ridiculous, sometimes wonderful, love affair with the land, and, like all voyeurs, they thrilled to the tale of someone else's wins and losses.

I give you back your white world of
ghostly tracks and perfect silence
Give me back the girl who once loved,
the crystal human sound of echoed laughter.

Looking back on my writing career—if I dare to suggest that having intercourse with words, teasing nouns, flirting with adjectives, and seducing verbs might be considered a career—I'd have to say that the secret of my modest success was a kind of innate and simple honesty. "The land is honest in her undertakings," I once wrote. "She never lies." What else could I hope to offer in my poetry and my stories except the same kind of unabashed and unashamed candor? It was as easy and natural to me as breathing: this is what I see and hear, taste and smell. This is what I feel, so this is what I write. While I admit that I love the flirty fun of trying to have my way with words, it never dawned on me that I might also be seducing a readership. By telling the plain truth of what was happening in my everyday, if not so ordinary, life, I was accidentally tapping into the huge collective unconscious of people who also longed for their own passionate connections.

There was a time when love of the land was enough.
The land gave life, took life, and all,
child and grandfather alike,
knew that love of the land was all there was.

While the West and I wrestled one another's spirits through the cycle of seasons—blizzards stacked upon snowstorms, unrelenting droughts when I prayed and bargained hard for rain, through weeks of rain when the hay was down, through early frosts that killed the garden and late squalls that killed the calves—the men who granted me access to untamed landscapes had their hands full with a teenage dreamer who resisted growing up, a temptress who was by turns testy or sultry, a restless workaholic who didn't know the meaning of downtime, and an obsessive cleanliness nut in a world of dust-laden wind, manure-caked boots, and cobwebs that bloomed in every old-log corner. Thinking of these men, I sympathize. They wooed a wildflower and ended up with a thorn-spiked gooseberry bush, alternately tender and sweet, or green-berry hard, sour, and bitter. While I try never to outright bash the men who provided the proverbial roof over my head and bacon on the table, I confess to lashing out, accusing them of the greatest of all sins: silence. I have harbored unkind and unhealthy thoughts regarding their inability to accommodate my impassioned nature. I suspect now that they knew of my unfaithfulness, that in some vulnerable, sore, and throbbing place in their supposedly tough hearts they realized they were not first in mine. They knew that that special space was occupied by a presence more powerful, more wild and independent, more stubborn and silent, more inaccessible and impossible than they might ever be. Who could blame them, finally, for alienating me when I had nothing left to offer but mere crumbs of leftover amor and affection because I spent my time mooning and daydreaming, fantasizing and writing about my phantom lover, the West.

> Come to me in silence
> and let your lips sing
> again our old song
> using my whispered name
> as sad, soft refrain.

I encountered the first fox in late fall just a few months after my husband of twenty years and I had separated. Walking to the Woodland Park post office in an early-season squall, blinking away snowflakes, I saw a young fox trotting toward me apparition-like in the whiteout. I stopped dead still on the sidewalk. She never faltered. Her ears perked, but she never slowed or paused. She came within five feet of me, leapt to the top wire of a yard fence, balanced there on bunched paws for a precarious second, then dropped to the ground on the other side and trotted to a run-down board-and-batten shed. She glanced back over her shoulder, slid beneath the structure, and disappeared. If not for her tracks in the snow, I might have labeled her vision or dream.

I stayed in the same spot, stunned, mesmerized more than anything else by her extreme grace, her ability to conquer obstacles as if they were not there: a human being in her path, no problem; a fence to jump, easily done. In the midst of civilization, she had found a place to shelter herself in the storm. And, from the looks of it, she traveled alone. Was there any reason why I couldn't do the same?

If the years I spent on the land taught me anything, they taught me that there is no way of knowing what tomorrow brings, that words like security and certainty don't exist in the real world. Dependent on the whims of weather, I never knew from day to day what I'd do and that, by the way, is a good corollary to the writing way of life. The Muse is as unpredictable as the weather. The moment I think I have her figured out, excepting sunshine, warm temperatures, and a conciliatory exchange, she turns her back on me and spits out a storm of lightning-laced hail. I can't plan ahead or forecast. All I can do is wait, be patient, and hope her mood changes so I can get back to work again.

Minding the Muse
Each word I write from this time on
will be a kiss born of her bids
a hesitant brush above the brow
or mingled breath on closed and quivering lids. . . .

As open and wet as false felt spring
and sleepy sad as autumn's eyes,

each word I write will be a kiss
that begs, delights, then dies.

"Why poetry?" someone once asked me. "I don't know," I answered.
"It's just the way the words come to me."

I don't think the words, I feel them. I see images the words represent. I hear them, smell them, taste them, then there is nothing else to
do except that I must touch them, feel them, explore them, know them.
Writing, for me, does not begin with an idea. It is not an element born
in the intellect. Writing begins with a sensation, something that nudges
or tingles or stabs. It is heart work, birthed through the laborious pangs
of emotion. Of course, once an image is pushed out of a pen and onto
the page in a hot and bloody rush of orgasmic pleasure that borders
on pain, then I call in the mind's steady, careful hands to clean up the
mess. Without the work of intelligent thought to get rid of the gore,
wipe up the mess, throw out the trash, and bundle the words up in a
tidy and orderly fashion, then there is nothing but miscarried sentiment whose proper fate is a solemn and decent burial.

Walking saves nothing
but puffs of chalk-white dust
rise around my ankles
like the dry buried breath
of long lost angels.

I write the same way that I live my life: I feel first, then think, and,
unfortunately, sometimes my mind doesn't do a very good job of cleaning up after my heart. Then, forced to wallow around in the carnage of
my own creations, I call in sympathetic colleagues or frustrated editors. As any other writer will confess, why I write and how I write is
one of the great unplumbed mysteries of my earthly journey. I write
because I have to: like breathing, eating, sleeping, making love, giving

birth, burying the dead, or worshipping the natural world. Talking about writing, or writing about writing, only spins me in a silly circle of attempting to understand something that cannot be understood. It can only be felt. It can only be accepted. It can only be honored and left to live its own cryptic and weird existence. Yet, I go on trying to express, explain, and comprehend.

> Stonecrop and cankerroot thrive
> on the rocky trail I walk at dawn;
> some things thrive on such small
> sustenance, so little soil.

On a midwinter day, when the backyard wore three feet of hard-crust snow, I lounged by Mom's sliding glass door leading onto the deck to watch an occult-spread of just-after-dawn rust light turn orange, then gold, as it burnished the uppermost branches of the ponderosa pine. Birds bolted from their breakfast at the feeder and a devil squirrel worrying a peanut in his front paws sashayed onto the wood rail as the red fox slid out of the shadows behind the shed. She nosed the frozen water dish, licked up a few bits of seed, turned a couple of circles in the snow snuffling for something more to eat, then honed in on the only patch of visible earth to be seen: a short oblong stretch of mat-ted grass beneath the bole of the tallest pine created by the afternoon sun melting back thin drifts under large overhanging branches. The red fox sniffed, scratched at the dung-brown grass, turned widdershins three times, then lay down, curled head to hip, her brushy tail cover-ing feet and nose so that the only things showing were eyes half-closed in a doze. The charmed light colored her cherry, then auburn, sorrel, chestnut, and dark palomino. I forced myself from the window and went back to work, but the fox remained most of the morning. Snug in a solar oven, she stayed until the sun shifted overhead and the radi-ant light no longer baked her into somnolent inaction. She provided a profound illustration, a tidbit of wisdom about life and about writing: take what you can from the moment, be glad and thankful, then move on.

> Stolen moments, I walk the night street
> alone, away from city lights 'til pavement
> turns to gravel, to grass. I stretch,
> fold to the night earth, face pressed to faded weeds
> and dirt, the frosted dew of autumn, the touch,
> the feel, the smell of everything left behind.

It became brief moments in time that I learned, slowly, to cherish my liaison with the West. I could not find a way to love something so big and mythic in character all at once. I could not take in the throbbing, overwhelming, incredible beauty of the land in one huge gulp. I had to teach myself to love in little sips, tasting this, then that. Nibbling the sight of spring's first bluebird. Savoring the burnt-lightning smell of a summer storm. Licking the last vestiges of autumn's tangy dying from my lips. Swallowing dry tough chunks of sorrow one at a time. Sucking on winter's ice to keep from dying of thirst. Chewing sweetness from the stalk of everyday walks. Masticating the meaning of wilderness out of the welter of human worries and concerns. With time, with the moments of seasons stacked upon the moments of years, I discovered that in the process of loving something that could not love me in return, I exhumed the intrinsic value of what I needed to love in myself.

> Wild, straw-swept, the worth
> of peaks and trees has ever been
> the movement of wing against wind,
> the sun across open, expansive sky,
> the old allure of patterned stars.

The Earth did not care if I lived or died. The West could give a hoot if I stayed or left. The wilderness would suffer her losses no matter how I mourned. The red fox would succumb to a dog in a fence corner or be caught in the glare of headlights in the middle of a two-lane highway. What began to matter was not who I loved or what I loved, but the act of loving, so like the art of writing, gave meaning and purpose to why I ended up in the West in the first place. I came because I was called to a place I needed to know in order to know myself. I stayed because I could not leave. I survived and taught myself to write because I needed to tell my stories, no matter how inept or imperfect or deformed at birth they were.

One evening at supper my Mom fussed about the fact that her planters under the bay window were being tipped over and messed with by some animal during the night. We guessed neighboring cats or loose dogs, perhaps even raccoons or skunks, though we'd seen none in months. We tried several things to prevent the minor damage and time-consuming clean-up, including putting mothballs around all the plants. Then, the woman who lived across the street solved the mystery for us. Just before first light, she told us, two foxes came to play on our porch—chasing tails, spinning circles, nipping and licking, and their raucous wrestling took its toll on the tidy approach to the house. Live traps to capture and remove the intruders came to mind, but I didn't want to displace the foxes. I felt that within a week or ten days, mating season would be over and the foxes would be about their business. The fact that they'd chosen Mom's covered walkway for a love-nest playground made me smile, made me hold close my thoughts of the new partner who had come into my life to wrestle with me in pre-dawn hours.

Since I couldn't grant myself an all-out infatuation with another wilderness landscape, perhaps I could allow my heart to run romantic and wild once again. I'd found someone who really wanted to hear my stories, who encouraged me to tell tales about my life as a backwoods stalker of the silences. An adventurous desert dweller, he was a man who didn't mind that I loved the land more than anyone or anything else.

> An hour or two is never enough. Even offering
> one day diminishes the devotion the land so deserves.
> Until I plunge into giving everything, vulnerable,
> as naked and unashamed as her own soul,
> how can I say I love her?

I don't think I chose to become a writer. Life cast a wide loop of unforgettable images in my direction and I stepped into the snare. The western landscape's distance-eating riata, tied off hard and fast, dragged me, not unwillingly but certainly full of apprehension, to a covert corral in a box canyon where heroines are held hostage until they surrender to the rogue's advances, to the place where mavericks are claimed and branded. Marked with weathered skin and wrinkled brow, scars on my heart, and the consumptive look of someone who has birthed countless stillborn poems and stories, I have lived to see surviving progeny go out into the world and touch other lives. Everything in life exacts a toll and I'm trying to learn to pay the price of my unrestrained loving without whining. If having a heart that looks like a road map is the cost of coquettish behavior and consenting to star-crossed encounters, then I will investigate new ways to use scotch tape, duct tape, super glue, pine tar, or anything else that will hold me together long enough to experience the last tasty tidbit the West has to offer.

> My future blooms before me like a sepia dream:
> withered, I roll and roll out of control
> toward some empty horizon,
> until, snagged in a sagging rusty wire, I hang,
> a sorry skeleton, but, oh, how stunning
> I'll look naked in starlight

Someone once said to me, as if scolding me for some unforgivable sin, "How can you stand to bare your soul and expose your heart in your poetry?" My response was, "How can I not?" When a lover whispers *take off your clothes*, it's hard to say no. When a lover asks you to skinny-dip in the river or dance naked in front of the fire, how can you bear not to join in? When a lover says *take my hand and run wild with me*, how can you turn your back and say I'd rather stay home? If I have stripped myself down to flesh and bones in order to tell the truest story I can tell, then I suffer shivering in the cold or the embarrassment of being vulnerable, but I also venerate the essence of what it means to be alive in a landscape that is still, at its elemental core, wild and untamed. I have never quite been able to see the sanctity of becoming overcivilized, of holding myself back from the primitive joys that unite me to my origins.

"You never lose by loving," said Barbara DeAngelis. "You always lose by holding back." It's just as easy to profess, "You never lose by writing what you feel; you always lose by censoring yourself."

"A Sensualist's Apology"

There is no air that others breathe
To satisfy my gasping lungs,
Or sound of air, reward of voice
To justify my seeking tongue;
The ache is not of mind or heart
The light and dark that draw apart,
It stems from someplace deeper still
In blood and bone, the soul of will,
To lead me down a different trail . . .
Where earth becomes my lover's arm
And sun my simple shield from harm.

By late winter I had only those two sightings of the red fox to imprint in my memory. I spotted her tracks in various places, but she had become elusive and invisible during the day. Perhaps she was holing up to avoid the cold, semihibernating until more food could be found. Then, one noon-time I glanced up from my desk work to see her sitting sedately in the driveway looking around as if she'd just woken from a Rip Van Winkle nap. The dog two houses away set up a raucous howling bark that was enough to shock the block. I expected the red fox to hightail back into the cover of nearby brush, but she simply stretched, yawned, trotted across the street toward the dog, leapt onto a chain-link fence, balanced her way down its length, and hopped onto a tall woodpile just twenty feet from the insane, slobbering beast who crashed against his pen in a repeated attempt to get through the wire and attack the piece of free-to-roam fur in its yard. Red fox yawned again, turned a casual circle, and lay down on the logs in a beam of strong sun shooting through the aspen trees. The dog continued to wail, cussing its frustration to the world, while the red fox, knowing she was safe, had the audacity to sleep.

> A woman could wait a lifetime
> for this kind of beatitude:
> tiptoe, sinking my tongue into
> a snowy mound atop a fence post
> my hands grip white wires
> and stretch into ecstasy.

As my writing escaped the boundaries of freelance articles and poetry, stretching into essays, memoir, and my first novel, *Side Canyons*, I began to discover that I had limited myself by believing that my love affair with the land would only survive if I was in close, daily, intimate contact with remote, secluded landscapes. It was my trip to the Grand Canyon several years ago that opened my heart to the notion that I might be able to love other wild places besides those right outside my own back door. It was my new partner in creative adventure who fueled this notion of being in love with numerous places by taking me backpacking in the Wichita Mountains of Oklahoma and the Guadalupe Mountains of Texas.

And it was the red fox who convinced me that I just might be able to find a way to be content in a brick house on a paved street tucked among aspens and pine in a subdivision of a small town not that far from a big city. Contentment thrives wherever you find it, happiness happens wherever you make it, love wherever you are willing to risk adventure.

"Where there is great love," Willa Cather said, "there are always miracles." The miracle for me as a writer is this: if I love the West and I love writing, then I have all that I ever really needed.

Early summer sprinkled the backyard with colorful wildflowers the last time I saw the red fox. Gaunt, her ribs showed. Her coat had shed off dull and raggedy, her alert ears and bright eyes showed me she was all right. Pendulous full dugs swung from her belly. Still favoring her hurt paw, she rushed in a slinky trot through fully leaved aspens toward the darker recesses of a neighboring patch of woods, probably on her way to feed a batch of kits after foraging all morning. She didn't stop or even pause when she noticed me on the deck putting out peanuts for the squirrels.

She did however, shake her head and slurp her tongue, thereby giving me the perfect profile of a confident, secure-in-her-own-world-and-on-the-way-to-better-things survivor. I gave her a small salute as she disappeared behind a wall of yellow-flowered wild clover against the fence. She made me smile. She would always make me smile.

I asked life's toughest question over and over again,
but the answer, whispered back, is always the same:

Love with an open hand,
release the wild geese you've sheltered and saved all summer
into the autumn sky to see if they can fly,
grant permission for every living thing to survive or die.

Though the West has innumerable critics pounding at her doors and clownish buffoons begging for attention, an unending line of true admirers waiting to pay court, and satisfied lovers too many to count, the West belongs to me and I belong to the West.

The tenuous love affair begins to feel more like a marriage, troubled at times, thrilling at others, but assuredly a union destined to last. Sometimes I have to be patient and wait my turn for an opportunity to sneak off for a clandestine meeting with wild places. But, somehow, I now know that when I long to be loved, to be accepted for who I am, yearn for communion, fight for understanding, demand recognition for my intense emotion and passionate temperament, I can fall into the open arms of a waiting landscape and allow myself to be taken away.

You and me we are the same
I prayed for you and you came–
and you stayed–
take me away
glass-eyed paint in the rain.

The land, the West, forever waits to be discovered anew. I promise to volunteer, over and over again, to sacrifice my sanity and risk my heart to be a devoted lover and ardent explorer, believing that, best of all, each anxious encounter will conceive a poem or worthy story. ∪

The West of Ghosts

Margaret Coel

M argaret Coel is the author of ten mystery novels set among the Arapaho Indians on Wyoming's Wind River Reservation. Her novels have received wide recognition and have been on the best-seller lists of several newspapers, including the *New York Times. The Spirit Woman* won both the Colorado Book Award and the Willa Cather Award for Best Novel of the West. It was also a finalist for the Western Writers of America prestigious Spur Award for Best Novel. *The Shadow Dancer* was a finalist for the Colorado Book Award.

Coel is the author of numerous short stories published in anthologies and articles that have appeared in such publications as *American Heritage* and the *New York Times.* She has also written

Margaret Coel
(Photo by Heidi Mack)

four nonfiction books on the history of Colorado. Her book, *Chief Left Hand*, a biography of an Arapaho chief and a history of the Arapahos, published in 1981, is still in print and has been included among the best one hundred books on Colorado history.

Coel is a fourth-generation Coloradan and grew up in Denver. She currently resides in Boulder where she writes from a study that looks out over the Rocky Mountains. A herd of deer graze on the hill outside her window and from time to time a mountain lion will wander past. "Every day," she says, "I drink in the West."

On the wall of my study is a framed, bronze-toned illustration by Frank McCarthy, titled *Beneath the Cliff of Spirits*. Six Shoshone warriors are riding across the lower half beneath stark cliffs emblazoned with petroglyphs. Both riders and ponies are painted and the warriors brandish spears partly wrapped in leather thongs to which are tied eagle feathers that wave overhead. Eagle feathers also sprout from their headdresses, but the dominant warrior wears the head of a gray wolf signifying that he is the leader of the scouts, like the alpha wolf, scouting the prey or the enemy.

The petroglyphs represent the spirits of the ancestors, and native people will tell you that they are chiseled by the spirits that dwell in the rock. The spirits manifest their presence by making the petroglyphs visible when they choose and to whom they choose. If you have ever gone looking for petroglyphs among the remote cliffs and rock formations in the West, you know that sometimes they can be seen and other times, even when you are certain they are present, they remain invisible. What makes McCarthy's illustration so powerful is that the spirits have obviously chosen to show themselves to the warriors. They ride alongside and float above, always nearby.

The illustration captures my own sense of the West where I was born and have spent my entire life—the Rocky Mountains and the vast, still mostly empty plains of Colorado. My West is a place of ghosts, a place where the ancestors hover nearby. It is a multilayered place with the present rooted in the past and the past always working its way into the present. Past and present—two sides of the same coin. It's possible to look at only one side, say the present, which might seem a rational approach, but the past is still there, shaping the heft and size, the depth, the overall configuration. This is the West that I try to bring to life in my novels and short stories, in nonfiction books, articles, and essays, the West that McCarthy so eloquently brought to life in the illustration.

That ghosts from the past inhabit the West seems obvious. The past is everywhere. It is part of the landscape from the high mountain valleys to the bluffs and arroyos that break up the plains. It is even part of the highways and roads. The multilane, congested I-25 on which a never-ending stream of cars and semis move up and down the Front Range of the Rockies from the southern reaches of New Mexico to the northern part of Wyoming follows an Indian trail. For two hundred years, Arapahos and Cheyennes rode the trail up and down this Front Range. They made the trail, those people of long ago.

There are other old Indian trails that have metamorphosed into highways and hundreds of two-lane roads that wind through the mountains and shoot across the plains, following the rivers, or what passes for a river in this part of the West but is often nothing more than a dry stream bed. Out on the plains, the roads run past clusters of cottonwoods where Arapaho and Cheyenne villages once stood, and probably the camps of Sioux, Kiowa, Apache, and Pawnee hunting parties. It is possible to imagine the white tipis sheltering in the shade of the trees, the sound of babies crying, dogs yapping, and horses neighing in the corrals. Or to imagine the warriors riding across the horizon on their way back to the village after the hunt.

There are stretches of ranchland across the plains, open, wind-blown places with a scattering of sagebrush and a few dried, gnarled trees. They probably look the same as they did when the warriors rode out to fight an enemy or hunt buffalo, or when soldiers attacked a village. Such a place is the site of the Sand Creek Massacre in southeastern Colorado, where the Third Colorado Regiment attacked the Cheyenne and Arapaho village in the freezing dawn of November 29, 1864. When the attack ended, at least 160 Indians, mostly women and children, lay dead. The elders say that one can still see the spirits of the women and children running through the thin stand of trees at the site, frantic to escape the soldiers bearing down on horseback.

In November 2000, Congress passed a law designating the more than twelve thousand acres on which the Sand Creek Massacre occurred as a National Historic Site, a piece of the past to be preserved for the future. Eventually the National Park Service will build an interpretive center where people can learn about what happened there and why it mattered, where people can touch the past as they do at the site of the Battle of the Little Big Horn.

In my West, such places are everywhere. They number in the hundreds, and I have visited many of them. They are the places that inspire me in my writing, the places where I can *feel* the past. Take the confluence of the South Platte River and Beaver Creek near the town of Brush in northeastern Colorado. Every summer, the Arapaho held a trading fair on the site. Tribes came from the north and south to barter and exchange goods—ponies and buffalo robes, tin pots, glass beads, Mexican silver and serapes, bolts of trade cloth, tobacco. Visiting went back and forth among the tipis, an exchange of news and gossip, the kids romping together. There is something about the site today—the gurgling creek, the wind brushing the leaves of the cottonwoods and the lone black bull that sometimes grazes the wild grass—that retains the exuberance of those gatherings, as if the Indians had just packed up the tipis and trading goods and ridden away. It is the feel of a stadium after the crowd has departed.

A couple of years ago I set out with my husband George to locate the place where the Arapaho Chief Left Hand had died and was buried. My first book, *Chief Left Hand*, published in 1981, was both a biography of this English-speaking diplomat and a history of his turbulent times. Left Hand became prominent in the mid-1800s during the time of the Colorado Gold Rush when nearly two hundred thousand Americans scrambled onto the empty plains and into the mountains expecting to scoop up gold nuggets that lay scattered at their feet, wash chunks of glittering gold out of the streams, and head back east wealthy men. The reality turned out to be different. They soon discovered that the gold, silver, lead, tungsten, molybdenum, and other minerals that would eventually be mined in Colorado were embedded in hard rock deep inside the mountains and that more than pickaxes would be needed to dislodge the riches.

The influx of gold seekers changed the lives of the Arapahos and Cheyennes on the plains and the Utes in the mountains in ways that the Indians could not have imagined. After the gold rush came home-steaders fencing off land for farms and ranches. Wagons and animals of the overlanders clogged the trails, tent settlements and tar-paper and plank-board towns sprang up literally overnight, army troops rode out from newly built forts to protect the newcomers from the depredations of Indians whose lands they had taken, and iron rails were laid across the plains and through the mountains, black smoke from the locomotives belching into the air. All of this squeezed the Cheyennes, Arapahos, and Utes into smaller and smaller areas until, finally, after all of the skirmishes, battles, and massacres, the survivors found themselves on reservations, the "reserved" portions of their own once vast lands. As one Arapaho put it at the time, the Indians thought that all the white people in the world had come to their lands.

In the four years I spent researching *Chief Left Hand*, I was able to locate evidence never before published that he had been mortally wounded during the Sand Creek Massacre but had made his way north with a handful of survivors to a large Sioux camp on the Smoky Hill River where he died. Left Hand was buried in the ground there, according to the Arapaho way.

By the time the book was published, I had visited most of the places where Left Hand had lived his life, but it was not until ten years later on a ninety-degree day in August, that I found the place where he had died. Today it is part of a ranch near the small town of Cheyenne Wells, Colorado.

After obtaining permission from the owner to scout the site where the camp once stood, George and I bumped over dirt roads in our Blazer raising clouds of dust. When we ran out of road, we got out and started walking. It was about noon, the sun white-hot overhead. All around us the glass-blue sky dipped over the empty, endless plains horizon.

As we trekked along, we realized we were not alone. Flying with us, perching on the little sand hills and clumps of brush, watching from no more than twenty or thirty feet away, was a large, wide-eyed owl. Apart from an occasional prairie dog or the buzzing of a bee, there was no other sign of life.

We veered in one direction, then another, hoping to stumble onto the Smoky Hill River, which we knew would be nothing more than a dry streambed. No matter how many zigzags we took, the owl stayed with us. The afternoon wore on with no sign of the riverbed, but instead of feeling anxious, I felt only peace. The Arapahos say that the ancestors may choose to accompany you on your way, and if they do, they usually assume the form of an owl. I had no doubt that somewhere in the glare of the sun and the sameness of the brown plain, we would stumble onto an indentation like a scar running across the land that would lead us to the site of the Sioux camp.

We found the riverbed and followed it to the wide bend where the camp had been located. We knew from the old records that the river had bent around it, but we hadn't known that the channel bent around a bluff and that the camp had been on top. From a distance on the plains, the cuts and rises in the land meld into the vastness.

We started hiking up the sliding dirt slope, the owl already perched on the edge above. When we reached the top, we stood perfectly still, unable to speak, hardly able to breathe. Rising above the plain that ran as far as we could see in every direction was a field of wildflowers— yellows, purples, reds, oranges, blues, vermilions, and whites—that swayed against the blue sky. It was there that Left Hand had died, and there, somewhere among the wildflowers, his body lay buried.

When we looked around, the owl was gone.

Not all of the ghosts in my West are Arapaho, however, or other Indians who lived on the plains and in the mountains of Colorado. There are the ghostly trails of trappers, people like Jedediah Smith and Jim Beckwourth who made a living of sorts trapping beaver in the streams. There were traders like the entrepreneurial Bent brothers—William and Charles—who, in 1830, established Bent's Fort, an adobe structure on the Arkansas River and the first permanent structure in United States territory west of the Great Plains. Santa Fe, still part of Mexico then, was already two hundred-twenty years old, already filled with its own ghosts of Spaniards, Mexicans, and Indians who settled the place and whose descendants moved up and down the Santa Fe Trail with wagon trains full of trade goods, always stopping at Bent's Fort.

A few years ago, I spent an evening at the reconstructed fort after the enormous gates had swung shut on the last tourist, leaving the fort to the imaginations of a group of western history buffs. We ate dinner in the courtyard with campfires burning, buffalo meat sizzling on a grill, Mexicans in sombreros strumming guitars, and the last of the summer sun flaring red on the adobe walls. It was easy to imagine that the present and past had traded places, that we were now caught in the past, that all around us were traders who'd come from Santa Fe or St. Louis or an Indian village, speaking a medley of languages, their horses grazing on hay in the corral, and William Bent himself upstairs in the corner room entertaining Kit Carson with a game of billiards at the only billiard table west of St. Louis.

There are also the ghostly trails of the gold seekers who clambered through the mountains, cutting burro roads high above the timberline up and over jaw-dropping steep peaks. One can hike to the top of those peaks and look down over miles and miles of old roads still visible in the fragile tundra and imagine the burros straining at the head of wagons loaded with ore that might contain a little gold, or might not. One can see the century-old tailings still spilling from mines cut into the sides of rock-strewn mountains so formidable that you wonder how anyone reached them. Yet, the gold seekers made the roads and sunk the mines in feats of daring and endurance that can only be a tribute to the power of greed or to the depth of the desperation that drove them on.

Traces of the old narrow-gauge railroads still cling to the mountains—roadbeds no wider than a wagon, switching back and forth on themselves as they wind higher and higher before plunging down the other side. One can well imagine the Denver, South Park, and Pacific trains churning through the Alpine Tunnel at five miles an hour, ferrying cars of gold, silver, and coal through the mountains.

Even the cities I know best are shaped by the past. I'm a city girl, raised in Denver, a sprawling city of freeways and suburbs and skyscrapers. I would argue that Denver would not be Denver without its ghosts.

Take the spit of land at the confluence of Cherry Creek and the Platte River on the edge of downtown, crowded with trendy shops and blocks of warehouses turned into upscale lofts and condominiums where bankers, lawyers, and software engineers live. On that same spit of land stood an Arapaho village within shouting distance of the tent and log cabin towns of Denver and Auraria. They were traders, the Arapahos, the "businessmen of the plains," the newcomers called them, and they wanted to live near their business just as, I suspect, many of the people in today's condominiums want to live near downtown.

Consider the variety of people who came west, settled in the new town of Denver, and left their personalities forever stamped on the city; the cowboys who drove the cattle down Denver's dirt streets to graze in pastures in the middle of town; the gunslingers like Doc Holliday and Wyatt Earp; the gamblers and flim-flam artists like Soapy Smith who ran the games of chance on Larimer Street, which is now a restored historical district of boutiques and restaurants.

There were people like Molly Brown, whose husband J. J. struck gold in Leadville, confounding all the experts who said it was a silver city, which it was, and would remain a silver city, which it didn't.

The stone lions still grace the mansion that J. J. built for Molly on Pennsylvania Street.

There was Henry C. Brown, no relation to Molly. Henry and his wife had traveled by wagon on the overland trail from the Midwest and stopped in Denver, intending to rest before crossing the mountains and continuing on to the California gold fields, their real destination. When Mrs. Brown awoke on her first morning in Denver under a sky as big as the outdoors and of the clearest blue she could imagine, she said to Henry, "You may proceed to California, Mr. Brown, if such be your wish. I shall remain here." Henry decided that he would also remain. He would go on to build the Brown Palace Hotel, a still elegant visitor from the past that has stayed on.

Such visitors can be found everywhere in Denver. The white-bricked Tivoli Building, for example, with its blue-tiled roof, built by German immigrants more than a century ago, still looming like a Bavarian castle over today's Auraria campus near downtown; the spire of the Daniels and Fisher Tower, nineteen stories high and soaring above the city in 1911, the highest building then on the Great Plains and a recreation of the Campanile in Venice, proving to the world that Denver was a city of culture, not just a cow town.

The dome of the state capitol shone at the other end of Sixteenth Street, a dome paved with real gold, an exterior built of granite, an interior decorated with red and white marble, all spewed out of Colorado's mountains. Such a grand building would symbolize the best of Colorado, a gift from the nineteenth century to future generations. It took almost two decades to finish the capitol, with every penny accounted for and no hint of corruption or scandal—an astonishing accomplishment for government officials in the Gilded Age. Indeed, in any age.

Out of the parade of such westerners—builders, gold seekers, traders, cowboys, and Indians, characters with personalities larger than life, the Molly Browns and Henry Browns, the Indian chiefs—the myth of the West grew up, helped to maturity by the writers of pulp novels and the movies of John Ford.

It has always seemed to me the myth of the West was about freedom. Where else could people be free enough to test their own mettle, to prove the stuff they were made of without the social constraints of propriety, the accepted wisdom that life should be lived in prescribed ways? In the wide open spaces of the West, waiting to be conquered, developed, and stamped with personality, one could figure out one's own way to live. Where else could Custer have been free to plunge headlong into his last battle? Or railroad magnates push the tracks of a transcontinental railroad through the wilderness one mile each day, no matter the weather and damn any other obstacle? Or J. J. Brown and H. A. W. Tabor, the silver king, and hundreds of other poor men get rich quick?

Where else could women vote in the nineteenth century except Wyoming, Colorado, Idaho, and Utah? Where else could women acquire their own land except by homesteading what was often the hardest-scrabble land available after men fenced off the best sections? But it was land women could own outright, their piece of independence. Where else could women herd cattle, rope calves? For that matter, where else could women mount a horse and ride alone into the plains and mountains, as the St. Louis-bred Susan Magoffin had spent her day at Bent's Fort in 1846, leaving behind a journal that bursts with the exhilaration of being free for the first time in her young lady's life. Free. Free. Free.

But the myth of the Old West failed to take into account some uncomfortable facts, such as the decimation and near extinction of the American Indian, the rape and destruction of the landscape, the pollution of streams and rivers, the near destruction of entire species of animals including the buffalo and the wolf. All true, no doubt, and yet that myth of freedom, born out of the larger-than-life characters who settled the Old West, refuses to die. Perhaps the reason is that those characters were real.

We knew them. My family carts around an enormous bag of stories that we pass from generation to generation about a lot of western characters. Most of my ancestors trickled into Colorado in the 1860s and 1870s when bands of Indians could still be seen riding across places like South Park which, not long before, teemed with large herds of buffalo.

My father's family had moved from Pennsylvania as far west as a rock-strewn farm in Missouri. In 1883, my paternal grandfather was the last of my ancestors to reach Colorado. The miners, railroaders, cowboys, and the independent women were the people among which my family lived, worked, and prospered.

Back in Missouri, my great-grandfather had hoisted a rifle on the front porch of the farmhouse and ordered Cole Younger and his gang off the land. That was prior to 1876 when Younger's attempt to rob a bank in Northfield, Minnesota, landed him in prison for the next twenty-five years. A great aunt was a longtime friend of Molly Brown's. I have a photograph of my mother's father as a young man, posing with three other young men, all dapper and well-scrubbed and cocky-looking, staring into a bright future. Three of them would hit it rich in the gold mines and establish families whose names are still found in Denver's social register, but my grandfather wasn't one of them. I remember the tobacco-spitting, leather-faced cowboys at the stock shows and rodeos we attended and the old timer who had worked with my father's father on the narrow-gauge railroads, then spent years tearing up the rails after the mines closed and the railroads went bust. I remember tales of mountain lions and bears he'd fought off to bring the rails out of the mountains.

In one way or another, the ghosts of these western characters trail through the different kinds of stories that I've written over the last twenty-five years. I started my career as a journalist, chronicling the accomplishments and the peccadilloes of modern characters for a weekly newspaper in a Denver suburb. I then contributed articles on the West to national newspapers and magazines such as the *New York*

Times, Christian Science Monitor, and *American Heritage of Invention and Technology.* In everything that I wrote, I was drawn to the past. I wanted to evoke the past that had formed my own imagination, not a country of dead people that the rest of us can hurry by, but a country that seemed alive and still mattered. I wanted to write about how our past shaped who we are in the West, why the past matters.

I have always followed the old maxim preached to every aspiring writer: write what you know. I write about a West that I know in my bones, that I've been breathing in since I drew my first breath, a West of stories intertwined with stories of my own family. Yet, I was drawn to writing about the Plains Indians about whom I knew very little. They seemed so attuned to the past. After all, it is the Cheyenne and Arapaho elders who see the women and children still fleeing the soldiers at Sand Creek. I decided to follow a contradictory maxim: write what you don't know, because then you will have the pleasure of finding out.

I wanted to find out about the Plains Indians. The more I learned about the tribes that had moved through Colorado—Cheyenne, Sioux, Kiowa, Apache, Pawnee, Arapaho—the more interested I became in the Arapaho. I liked the way they raised their children. They called their method "the easiest way," which meant talking to them, explaining how the world worked, why it was good to do one thing and not another. I liked the mixture of practicality and the deep spirituality that saw all creatures, including the two-leggeds and the wingeds, as relatives, all connected to one another. I liked the ideal of living in beauty. Even the simplest tools or items of clothing should be beautiful, the women said, since they were seen every day. I liked the way they taught their children to live in harmony with one another and the Earth. Did the Arapahos always live those ideals? Of course not. They are people, not saints. They stumbled and fell like everybody else, but what was important was that they never gave up on their ideals.

Everything I read about the Arapahos in the mid-1800s, the time of the gold rush, mentioned one of their leaders, a man named Left Hand, a man fluent in English. I learned that only a handful of Plains Indians ever became fluent in English. They didn't have to learn English or any language other than their own. They used sign language to communicate with other tribes and with the traders and others coming onto the plains. Yet, Left Hand not only spoke English, I learned he spoke Cheyenne and Sioux. I set out to find out about a man who was interested enough in other people to learn their languages. What kind of man was he? Where were his villages? Which battles did he fight? How did he learn English? What became of him?

It was the finding out, the learning what I hadn't known, that resulted in the book *Chief Left Hand* and launched me into an adventure that continues today. I wrote other nonfiction books on the history of Colorado, with the ghosts of the gold seekers, railroaders, and builders all making their presence felt, but I kept returning to the Arapahos, where the lines between past and present seemed blurred, one melting into the other. When Arapahos from the Wind River Reservation in Wyoming head south to visit relatives in Oklahoma, they go by way of Sand Creek to pray for the people who died there. The Sand Creek Massacre took place 142 years ago, but to the Arapahos it still matters.

Ten years ago, I happened to hear Tony Hillerman speak about writing mystery novels set among the Navajos. I remember sitting in the middle of a large conference room surrounded by other writers and thinking that I might write a mystery novel set among the Arapahos. It would be a contemporary novel, I remember thinking, but it would also be about the past. It would be both sides of the same coin.

This seemed like a good idea. I did not know how to go about writing fiction but I liked reading mystery novels. They were fun to take to the beach or curl up with in the evenings. How tough could one be to write? I was going to find out, but not before I figured out what I would write about. For inspiration, I began digging into my research for *Chief Left Hand* and came upon something that had taken place when the Arapahos and Cheyennes were moved to reservations. I only mentioned it in *Chief Left Hand*, but I remembered being stunned and angry by the information. I knew that someday I would write more about it. It became the basis for the plot for *The Eagle Catcher*.

What I'd uncovered was this: Soon after the treaties that sent the tribes to the reservations were signed—the Arapaho and Cheyenne chiefs making their X's on the word of government translators who assured the chiefs that they were signing what they thought they were signing— the government sent out agents to "make the reservations ready for the Indians." The agents carried out the assignment by carving off the plains with water and timber for their own ranches and leaving the less desirable land for the tribes. This at a time when the Plains Indians had just been defeated in a war, huge numbers of their warriors dead, the buffalo dispersed and slaughtered, the children crying with hunger. This was the remnant that struggled onto the reservations: the wounded and demoralized, the old and sick and hungry. "We were a pitiful lot," is the way that Virginia Sutter, an Arapaho friend, described the nine hundred Indians who came to the Wind River Reservation in 1878.

The story I set out to tell in *The Eagle Catcher* was not just the history of how sections of the reservation lands were stolen, but the way in which crimes of fraud and deceit that occurred more than one hundred years ago echo through the present. My novels since have reflected the same theme: the ghosts of the past that hover around us. When I am looking for a plot for a new novel, I look into the bitter period between the time when the Arapaho roamed the plains, when they were free, and the early years on the reservation.

One of my novels, *The Story Teller*, is about the ledger books that the Arapahos, Cheyennes, Kiowas, Crows, and Sioux wrote. They wrote in pictographs, intricate and detailed, that filled the pages of the ledger books they had obtained in trade. They used crayons and pencils to tell the stories of battles and heroic exploits and the intimate accounts of village life. Two thousand Plains Indians ledger books, scholars say, once existed. Today there are fewer than three dozen, mostly in museums, some in private collections. A complete ledger book can be worth a million dollars. Pages razored out of them are also in museums, but they turn up from time to time in galleries and places like Santa Fe and Aspen. At least three pages are known to exist from a ledger book account of the Sand Creek Massacre.

For all my stories and novels, I start with questions of what if? For *The Story Teller*, the questions were: What if a complete Arapaho ledger book on the Sand Creek Massacre were found? What if the Arapaho tribe wanted to reclaim the book as part of their cultural and historical heritage? What if someone else wanted possession of the book, worth one million dollars? Out of the answers to these questions came the plot for a novel that wove the importance of the ledger books into our knowledge and understanding of past events like the Sand Creek Massacre.

I remember standing at the granite stone marking the grave of Sacagawea on the Wind River Reservation and asking myself: What if Sacagawea found her way back to her people after the Lewis and Clark expedition and lived to be an old woman, as the Shoshones and Arapahos believe? What if she had dictated her story to the wife of the government agent who wrote the story in a notebook, as historical records say happened? What if the notebook had been rescued from a fire at the agency instead of being destroyed? What would Sacagawea's account of the expedition be worth today? The answers became *The Spirit Woman*.

All of my other novels, *Wife of Moon, Killing Raven, The Shadow Dancer, The Lost Bird, The Thunder Keeper, The Dream Stalker, The Ghost Walker*, and the novel I am currently writing, were rooted in the past. With fiction, I am no longer limited to narratives of what might have happened. I can plumb the meaning and imagine how a past event might continue to affect individuals and families. In all that imagining, I believe every fiction writer would agree, it is astonishing how often we hit upon a kernel of truth and how often readers say: "How did you know that was how it was?" "How did you know we felt that way?" After publication of *The Lost Bird*, which dealt with the crime in the recent past of infants being stolen from reservations and sold on the black market, I received a call from an Arapaho woman. "You wrote my story," she said. "How did you know my story?" I didn't know her story. I had imagined how such a crime would affect everyone involved.

The stories that I imagine keep me moving between the past and the present: the past of the Arapahos on the plains and their life today on the reservation. I spend part of every summer visiting the reservation, catching up with friends, talking with people, and most of all, listening to what they have to say and the way in which they say it. George and I have driven the roads where my characters live, we've visited the sites that we write about. We've gone to the powwows and the rendezvous, we've taken part in the sweat lodge, we've sat and listened to the elders. We've attended the Sun Dance, and in all of this we have touched a past threaded through the present.

I remember the July day we came over a rise on Ethete Road on our way to the Sun Dance. Spread through a scattering of cottonwoods on the dance grounds below were several hundred tipis, white and gleaming in the sun. We stopped the Blazer and got out, struck by what we saw. We could hear voices carried on the breeze, the sound of dogs barking. People were moving about among the tipis, ducking in and out of the brush shades where food would be constantly available. In the center was the Sun Dance lodge, the sides fashioned from willow branches that the men had cut in the riverbeds, the scraped pole overhead, rainbows of cloth offerings tied to it and billowing against the blue sky. We might have been looking down on an Arapaho village in the Old Time about to begin the holiest of ceremonies, the Sun Dance.

As the Arapahos would say, the ancestors are always with us. ∪

Confessions of a Writer

Don Coldsmith

Don Coldsmith
(Photo by Terry Rhinehart)

Don Coldsmith is the author of forty books and nearly eighteen hundred weekly syndicated newspaper columns. There are over six million copies of his books in print, as well as British, French, German, and Russian editions. Coldsmith has been a combat medic in World War II, a youth director, gunsmith, taxidermist, physician, teacher, and rancher. He is the winner of a Spur Award for Best Paperback Novel, *The Changing* Wind, the Owen Wister Award for lifetime achievement in Western American literature, and was named the "Best Living Writer of Western Historical Novels" by *True West* magazine.

I'm often asked, "I suppose you've always wanted to write?"

The answer is no. I had not thought about writing much beyond assignments in school. I enjoyed those occasionally if the required topic was interesting.

I think most writers are readers first. As a kid, my favorite thing to do was to read. I learned to read in the lap of my grandmother before I started school. She wore bifocal glasses and followed the words with a fingertip. I could read just from watching before I even knew I could read.

I began to read everything available: newspapers, magazines, even cereal boxes. My dad, a Methodist minister, was expected to move every three or four years, and in one town where we lived, the library was within walking distance. So engrossed was I in the books that the librarian would have to send me home for supper sometimes. It was in that library that I realized with a shock that some books are better than others!

I continued to read, mostly outdoor adventure historical fiction such as Ernest Thompson Seton, James Willard Schultz, Zane Grey, James Fenimore Cooper, Mark Twain, and sometimes Jules Verne and Robert Louis Stevenson.

Another characteristic common to writers is that most of them tend to have a vast amount of personal experience at a vast number of unrelated jobs: cowboy, oil field worker, merchant marine, travel with the circus, and so on. The common denominator here is an inquiring mind, wanting to know what is around the next corner. Many of these writers-to-be, like myself, originally had no real aspiration to write, just to go out and "see the elephant." In truth, a writer friend did exactly that for a summer, traveling with a circus.

My own curiosity, or wanderlust, was aided and abetted by the onset of World War II. It was a few years after Pearl Harbor before I turned eighteen. In the meantime, I had volunteered for a Civil Defense unit, and had several jobs not usually available to teenagers, but were at the time due to the scarcity of men. I was a radio disc jockey, a deputy grain inspector, drove a delivery truck for a poultry and egg wholesaler, graduated high school, and took two semesters at the junior college in Coffeyville, Kansas.

My "greetings" from the president came in a letter when I turned nineteen. I was to report to the bus station for transport to Fort Leavenworth for induction into the army. To shorten a long story,

I was placed in basic training in "pack artillery," using mountain howitzers and pack mules, six mules to each 75mm gun.

By the time I reached a combat area as a replacement, however, they weren't using mules there. Mountain troops had been important in Europe, but the South Pacific was a different war. I was assigned to a combat unit and became a medic, learning on the job.

We were almost literally packing to invade Japan when the atom bomb ended the war and saved millions of lives, American and Japanese. One was mine.

Our unit entered Japan as one of the first, and was assigned to operate the Omori Prison Island, where they were incarcerating most of the staff grade Japanese prisoners of war. As combat medics, my partner and I were assigned to the daily medical care of about forty war crimes prisoners. Most were generals and admirals. There was also Prime Minister Hideki Tojo, Japan's major bad guy, and a scary-looking little man named Hashimoto, head of the Black Dragon Society, the traditional organization of professional assassins known as the Ninja.

I was a private, first class. I visited often with General Homma, the "Butcher of Bataan." He had been educated in England and was not trusted by his junior officers, who probably initiated many of the atrocities of the Bataan Death March to embarrass the old man. I thought he was getting a bad rap, and all of this was brought out later at his trial. Homma was the only war crimes prisoner executed with military honors, but that's another story.

In a few weeks, our combat unit, the 637th Tank Destroyer Battalion, was replaced by trained army of occupation troops and we moved on.

In another year or so, I was back home, attending college, and with a few more odd jobs. I worked as a gunsmith, a taxidermist, and for a short while on a construction job. My dad, now a district superintendent in the Methodist Church, needed some part-time preachers, so in my senior year of college I filled a couple of pulpits for him each Sunday, earning enough to keep tires on my 1936 Chevrolet.

My main summer job for several years, however, was as a camp counselor at Camp Wood, a YMCA camp in the Kansas tallgrass prairie Flinthills. This not only had a great influence on my life, but led to my first steady job as director of youth activities in the Topeka YMCA.

Four years later I was restless. I was beginning to get some job offers, but I saw that advancement led to administration. These jobs would put me behind a desk, doing paperwork. I had already had the outdoor recreation jobs which is where the fun happens, I realized.

I resolved to go back to school and try for another career. I needed one year to take the courses necessary to apply to medical school. I also needed a place to live and a part-time job. I had married and had a child by this time.

Then I heard of a small town with a Congregational Church that needed a part-time minister. They had a pretty good minister's residence, and it was fairly close to the University of Kansas. I preached for them a time or two, and we worked out a deal. I was granted authority to perform the Sacraments for one year, in that church in Tonganoxie, Kansas.

It worked out well. I commuted to classes, was preaching on Sundays, had a mail-order gunsmithing business in the basement, and worked as night man in the bait shop at the lake marina that summer. And, I was accepted into medical school for the next year.

There was one incident during my years in medical training that may have affected my later interest in historical fiction. I had an opportunity to visit with a delightful lady who was nearing the century mark in birthdays. Her mind was clear and sharp, and I realized that she might have some fascinating memories. The year was 1957.

I had a friend who had just acquired a new toy, a device that was soon to revolutionize the music industry: a tape recorder. This one was bulky and rolled a tape from one reel, six or seven inches in diameter, to another of the same size. He agreed to let me experiment with it. I concealed the recorder to prevent any undue distractions and simply sat and asked questions to keep her stories coming.

The result was about an hour of family stories and recollections. Some were humorous, some tragic, and you had everything in between. She even remembered when the president was shot. President Lincoln!

At the time, I had no ambition to write these stories, only to preserve them. In recent years, I've found them useful for background in historical settings. Some of her anecdotes have resulted in short stories, and I hope to use them even more.

To advance my own story a few years, we were living in the country outside of Emporia, Kansas. We were raising a few horses and five daughters—mine, hers, and ours, as it turned out. That, too, is another story. In such circumstances, we had several kids in 4H and were active in a local saddle club, composed mostly of cowboy and country types. Many were my patients in my practice of medicine. I had a broad family practice specialty, did some general surgery, and delivered babies, about three thousand of them before I quit to write.

Ray Call, the managing editor of the *Emporia Gazette*, the old family-owned William Allen White newspaper, had become a friend as well as a patient. Call had asked me to do a little "stringer" work for the *Gazette* on some of the 4H projects, which was easy and enjoyable.

Now, it must be noted that our horse operation was no high-dollar situation, more like a dirt-scrabble, low inventory thing. Make-do, patch it, use it up. Still, I was trying to do it right, and our successes in the show competition were on the right track with our necessarily low-budget efforts.

I was approached by the Appaloosa breed registry to serve as a regional inspector. Largely a nonpaying assignment, it was still a way to get away from the phone on my day off, travel at someone else's expense, and look at good horses. I began to develop theories and opinions about the horse industry. We were subscribing to several horse magazines, and I was a bit disappointed in some of the articles. There are people who know horses, and people who know writing, I realized, but these are not necessarily the same people.

I wrote a story about some of the offbeat and crazy things that had happened to us at the horse shows and sent it to one of the magazines. I was astonished to receive a check for thirty dollars. I realized I could sell this stuff, and I was hopelessly hooked. In retrospect, that's when I became a writer. It wasn't for the thirty dollars. It wasn't even for the thrill of seeing my name in print. Where we live you can accomplish that by merely running a stop sign. The thrill was seeing my *ideas* and *thoughts* in print, and realized that somebody thought enough of my ideas to read them.

In my meager spare time, I began to write for several of the major horse magazines, gaining a little name recognition. I kept quiet about my day job as a physician. (Sometimes it was a night job, too). In a year or so, I'd start getting phone calls from editors wanting to know if I could do an article for an upcoming edition and could I get it in by a certain date? I'd always try to accommodate.

There was also a small weekly newspaper in Emporia, the *Times*. Merle Bird, the editor, approached me with a request: Would I consider writing a weekly column about the area's horse activities, saddle clubs, shows, sales, races, county fairs, whatever? He could offer no pay—I knew his paper was struggling—and I didn't want to do it. But, Merle was a friend, as well as one of my patients. I asked the advice of the editor at the *Gazette*.

"Do it!" said Ray Call. "It will help your writing to have a regular deadline. Besides, one door opens another, and it's always something you hadn't even thought of when you took hold of the knob!"

Talk about a prophecy! I had no idea.

I still had my doubts. I really didn't think that there was enough material to support a weekly column, but I agreed to try. The first *Horsin' Around* column was dated September 1971, with the provision that I could stop at any time.

I've written one every week since. When there was nothing happening, I'd write about something else, or I'd pick up a story at the feed store or the sale barn. The *Emporia Times* folded within a year or so, but by that time I had another paper or two in Missouri carrying the feature.

Now self-syndicated, *Horsin' Around* has produced more than eighteen hundred weekly columns and three anthologies, collections of favorite essays. It's no longer just about horses, but general interest, humor, nostalgia, current events, family, and whatever comes along. It's even been quoted in *Reader's Digest*, a mossy old joke about a talking horse.

My magazine work was suffering for lack of time. But now, I was considering another possibility. The first *Horsin' Around* anthology had been well-received, and I was considering an ambitious goal. I had grown up listening to the stories of my grandfather, Ezra Willett. He had, as a young teenager, driven an ox team and covered wagon into Kansas to homestead. Maybe I could put some of his adventures into a novel.

I was still in a busy medical practice. I would need some help and advice, and I figured I knew where to go for that. I had a brother who was a *real* writer. He had been a war correspondent in Korea, had worked for the Associated Press, had been an editor for *World Book Encyclopedia*, and at that time had his own newspaper in Virginia, a time-honored weekly. He was the youngest child of four, and his family nickname was "The Varmint," despite my mother's objections. I knew that he could help me, and he was coming to visit us, a rare occasion in itself.

At the appropriate moment, when we were alone, I asked if he'd help me on a writing project.

"Sure, Don," said The Varmint charitably. "What is it? How can I help you?"

"Well, I'd like to write a novel, containing some of our grandfather's stories."

There was a long silence, and my brother's answer may have been responsible for any success I have had since in the literary field.

"Well, what the hell," he said. "I'd like to take out somebody's appendix some day"

I had to write.

That novel was seen by at least thirty publishers and was never published. It had some problems, which I recognized later, after some experience. I did use much of it, however, in one of my historical novels, *South Wind*.

Even in failure, however, that novel opened some doors. I was drinking coffee with a senior editor from Doubleday, who had already rejected it, and was telling him about the early history in our part of the Great Plains. Areas within two hundred miles of where we still live have been claimed by six modern nations—Spain, France, Mexico, the Confederate States of America, the United States, and the Republic of Texas. In addition, there were numerous American Indian sovereignty claims. We still find Spanish artifacts. Coronado led an expedition into Kansas in 1541, the first of many. Henry Hudson, the "discoverer" of the New York river that bears his name, had not even been born.

I mentioned having found a Spanish horse bit of early design, similar to that used by Coronado and others. I remarked that if it could talk, what a story that bit could tell. The editor put down his coffee cup, leaned across the desk, and said, very seriously, "Write me *that* story."

Trail of the Spanish Bit was my first published novel, in 1980. It involved a lost Spaniard, left behind when Coronado turned back in 1541. What would happen to him? He will freeze, the first winter, unless he takes up with the locals. It was necessary to research both the Spanish and Native American cultures to write it. I had determined that I would try to be as accurate as possible, historically.

Trail of the Spanish Bit was published as a Double D Western, a low-budget hardcover library edition. A *western*? I thought somebody had made a mistake, so I called my editor in New York.

"No," he reassured me. "It's a sort of trial balloon, to break out of the mold of the generic western. New time periods, new historical slant, better characterization. Let's face it. There are a limited number of times one may shoot it out in the street at the OK Corral. Eventually, we have to do something else."

I've thought of that many times since as the "western" has changed and grown, reaching for respectability.

I had no idea that in one of these changes, I'd find myself right in the middle. I had no ambition to write about Indians. I wanted to write about my grandfather and his problems on the frontier. I wanted to write about cowboys.

But to depict the Plains buffalo hunters in that first novel, I had to do the research. I couldn't determine what tribes Coronado might have encountered in 1541. I decided on a fictional tribe, one with cultural traits from several Plains tribes: Kiowa, Cheyenne, Comanche, Arapaho. Nearly any tribe's name for itself translates as "The People," or "Our People."

It was a lucky break. If the people in my story are nobody in particular, but a generic culture, they become *everybody*. I became astonished at the way my story was accepted by American Indians.

There was, perhaps, another reason. In writing about the West prior to this time, it had been customary to depict Indians as faceless "bad guys," bloodthirsty savages. In that first book, I had only one white Spaniard. All the other characters are natives. I had to depict them as *people* who laugh and cry and fall in love and worry about their teenagers, like all other humans.

My "Spanish Bit Saga" quickly became a series from the Indian point of view, and I was to live with it. I had originally thought of the Spanish bit story as a single novel about a lost Spaniard, but it took on a life of its own. The publisher asked for a sequel, then another. I wasn't even writing them in sequence. It was at about book number five when my editor asked me to make it a series, creating the "Spanish Bit Saga," tracing descendants of Juan Garcia throughout history. "And let's keep it in sequence," the editor said. Volume number thirty-two, in the spring of 2004, takes place about 1800. I'm currently working on the next one.

In 1983, the three finalists for the Western Writers of America's Spur Award for Best Western Novel were Terry C. Johnston's *Carry the Wind*, with strong Indian characters, Fred Grove's *Match Race*, about early quarter horse racing, and my novel, *Follow the Wind*, part of the series. Fred's novel, more traditional, won the Spur. But, it also depicted a part-Indian jockey as a major character.

Some years later, Jack Schaefer, author of *Shane*, noted that it was the year 1983 when it became acceptable to write about Indians. Twenty years earlier, he had written a novel, *The Canyon*, with all Indian characters, which was notably unsuccessful.

"The public just wasn't ready to read about Indians yet," Grove noted.

There have been other changes, but what an honor to be a part of that one. Of course, it changed my entire life. I'm identified with writing about Indians.

In 1988, I closed my medical office after thirty years. I wasn't yet of retirement age, but I needed more time to write. It was a career move. Still not full-time, though. We now have only one retired horse, but we raise cattle, about thirty calves a year. I do the physical work, with good reason: if I keep in shape this way, I don't have to jog or play golf. The joggers who trot past our house don't appear to be having much fun. I'd rather fix fence and haul hay. And, of course, write.

But what about *being* a writer?

I've heard it quoted that there are fewer than three hundred full-time freelance writers in North America, quite possibly an accurate estimate. Even among some of the big names, they'll have a vocation on the side to support their writing habit. When asked what advice he'd give to an aspiring writer, Elmer Kelton says, "Just don't quit your day job."

I'd modify that just a bit: Prepare to make a living some other way, and write without the pressure of trying to earn a living. My brother Varmint, for instance, could have been a great creative writer, but never did much beyond that required by his job and the time clock. When he'd written all day, it was hard to think about doing it some more in the evening. He died before he got around to it. His writing job prevented him from becoming a *creative* writer.

I once heard that there are three essentials to becoming a writer: First, *write* something every day; second, write *something* every day; and third, write something *every* day.

There's food for thought there.

I've also heard would-be writers worrying about "writer's block." Most of the more capable writers I know would laugh at the idea of writer's block. I personally have had the opposite problem. My head would be bursting with ideas, and I literally had to sit down and put pen to paper to get them all out. I had done the paragraphing and rewriting in my head a dozen times before I had the opportunity. A considerable portion of my first published novel, *Trail of the Spanish Bit*, was written on the backs of yellow hospital order sheets, in the hours before daylight, while I was awaiting the arrival of babies.

When working at a day job, and we wake up a bit draggy and unambitious, we can call in sick. If there's no one to report to, we have no excuse. To claim writer's block is only making an excuse not to write. Get real. Write *something*.

I still write in longhand. Many writers I know do at least one draft in longhand anyway. You're in a different mode, somehow. I did try dictation, briefly. I was an expert in dictation from my medical career, but for creative writing it was a complete disaster. I went back to my battered pencil.

I hand the pencil copy to my assistant, Ann, who has worked for me for more than twenty years. She operates my computer in her own basement office, and we have done more than thirty novels together. Granted, it's a crazy way to work, but we can turn out a quarter million words of book manuscript per year, besides my weekly syndicated column, correspondence, and some short stories and articles.

As the saying goes, "If it ain't broke, don't fix it."

My lack of academic credits in creative writing may have been an advantage. I've heard people discuss, seriously, how many different plot lines there are in literature. Three? Seven? Ten? I was once told by a highly successful novelist that there's really only one, the universal plot: *People*, striving toward a difficult *goal*, against tremendous *odds*.

This makes sense to me and allows a wide range of potential tales. Add on the thought that the story's striving may not always be successful.

Here's another thought, a purely personal preference: I like to have at least one character who, if not totally ethical, tries to be, at least part of the time. I guess I revert to the cowboy culture, good guys versus bad guys. For me, the so-called spaghetti westerns filmed in Italy with Clint Eastwood just didn't have it. There were really no good guys, just bad guys and worse guys. But, that's personal preference.

I mentioned earlier my strong feeling about historical accuracy. There are those who think it's not important when you're writing fiction. I could not disagree more. Unless we are writing fantasy or science fiction, it is important to relate the truth, what could have happened, historically. To do otherwise is not only intellectually dishonest, but misleading. To distort historic fact in the minds of young readers is unethical. Some writers, even some big names, get away with it but lose the respect of honest researchers.

Historically, what survives in the memory of any culture is not their technology, but their stories, the literature, including the fiction. This is an awesome responsibility.

My goal has always been that no one could prove that my story did *not* happen. I don't claim it did, just that it could have within the frame of history.

Closely akin to this is another theory of mine. Maybe the influence of my Native American themes shows through. To the Indian, everything has a spirit: a rock, a tree, all of Creation. Our own traditional culture denies that a *place* may have a spirit, yet we invalidate that by talking of a gloomy place, a happy or threatening or cheerful setting.

I would never write a scene and describe its setting without having been there to feel its spirit. For any scene I ever wrote, I could take you to that place. How else would I know how my characters felt, unless I'd been there to feel it? It also helps with description.

In writing about people, we usually have an individual in mind. A character takes on personality traits of someone we know. Their mannerisms, the way they walk, talk, react to events. To recognize and accept this is a great help.

I was advised by a respected elder among the writing fraternity, "Don't worry about a plot. Just develop two or three characters, think about them, how they move, how they react. Then, put them in the worst situation you can think of and see how the hell they get out of it."

It works. I've used it. A similar method involves some historical event involving great danger and tense situations. Then, drop the fictional characters into the middle of the fracas.

A time or two, I've *dreamed* a story line, awakened, and made a few notes, which otherwise I'd forget by morning. Each time, this has resulted in one of my better stories. I think the phenomenon may relate to the poet's Muse or guiding entity.

One of the most common questions asked of a writer is "Where do you get your ideas?" I don't know a writer who could tell you.

I once read a short essay about a writer who had died and gone to hell. Hell, for him, consisted of a white room with no furniture except a white desk with a typewriter and a chair. He was chained to the desk, and through eternity people walk through the room and ask him: "Where do you get your ideas?"

I've never seen it as a problem. It's been the other way, finding the time to put them all down on paper. It makes me think of an old Cherokee saying: "The world is filled with stories, which from time to time permit themselves to be told."

What would be a greater honor than to be one of those chosen to tell them? A writer.

Times change. The publishing world is an entirely different entity these days. Writers still write. It's a crazy business, but probably always has been. Surely, the storyteller was created along with spoken communication. We have our problems. It takes an understanding family to realize that when the writer sits for hours, staring out the window, he's *working*.

Why, then do we do it? Not for the money, in most cases.

A few years ago, several of us writers of the American West would sometimes set out on a homegrown booksigning tour. Usually, Terry C. Johnston was the initiator, our designated control freak, and he would phone the others. Several writers were involved at one time or another: Win Blevins, Earl Murray, Dick Wheeler, maybe another one or two. Terry would set up a tour, generally starting somewhere on Colorado's Front Range, hitting towns like Fort Collins and Loveland, then north into Wyoming and west to Idaho.

He had contacted bookstores in each town, setting up signings, so we had a tight schedule. You can imagine the astonished looks on the faces of readers in some of the small towns, and we were treated like royalty. We'd be out for about a week, and usually the wives, at least those who could, joined us. This led to some lasting friendships, of course, as well as selling a lot of books and getting a lot of exposure and name recognition.

We had all gone out to dinner one evening, in Cheyenne as I recall. It had been a good tour, and one of the men rapped on the table for attention. He had a question: If you had another way to make a living, and were not being paid for your writing, would you still write?

The response was instantaneous, almost in unison, and positive. More revealing was the tone of the voices which reflected, "Why would you even ask?"

Yes, I'm a writer. ∪

Robert J. Conley
(Photo by Evelyn Conley)

Accept the Mystery

Robert J. Conley

Robert J. Conley, Cherokee, was born on December 29, the anniversary of the murder of Thomas Becket in 1170, the birthday of Charles Goodyear in 1800, the first articulation of Thomas Jefferson's Indian Removal Policy in 1802, the birth of Andrew Johnson in 1808, of Albert Sydney Pike and William Gladstone in 1809, the signing of the Cherokee removal treaty in 1835, Texas statehood in 1845, and the massacre of the Sioux Indians at Wounded Knee. Conley is convinced this auspicious date has had some mysterious impact on his entire life.

Conley earned an MA in English at Midwestern State University in Wichita Falls, Texas, and began a teaching career in 1968, one that lasted nineteen years. He published his first novel in 1986, and since then has published seventy more, as well as a collection of short stories. He writes full-time and lives in Tahlequah, Oklahoma, the capital of the Cherokee Nation, with his wife Evelyn, who is also Cherokee.

Whenever I'm asked how I go about writing anything, I have to pause. I don't really know. Several years ago I quit teaching, and this was one of the main reasons. I could pick a textbook, have students read it, and I could teach according to it, but I was not being honest about it. I don't write the way the textbooks say one should write. In fact, I don't think I write any two projects in quite the same way.

I wrote my first novel almost before I knew what I was doing. I was angry about something I had been reading regarding Cherokee history. I was fresh out of graduate school and had my head pumped full of academic stuff, so my first impulse was to write a scholarly article that would tell the world the whole truth. I searched for the right research material to no avail. Then one day, out of frustration and anger, I sat down at my typewriter and started writing. I have no memory of having decided to write a novel. I was writing something to show the way I felt about a situation I had discovered in the false material that had been previously published about Cherokees. I finished that first novel without ever having made an outline or drawn up a plan of any kind. However, it took fifteen years and some revision before I could find a publisher for it. It finally came out from Doubleday in 1986 under the title *Back to Malachi*.

My first hard-learned lesson was that a writer without an agent has to figure out what an agent would be doing for him, if he had one, and then do it for himself. The second lesson I learned was that I could sell a second book on the basis of an outline. For my second and third books, I submitted outlines to Doubleday and then followed them, more or less. I also had a collection of short stories I had written during those long fifteen years, and I had written them in much the same way I wrote that first novel—no outline and very little plan. That collection was published by the University of Oklahoma Press, the first original fiction they ever published, with the title *The Witch of Goingsnake and Other Stories*. Since then I have written over seventy novels, most of them with my own name, some under another name. I have written some using outlines, some using only a one-page synopsis, some using a real life or some historic episode as an outline, and some just by starting the first page, or the first sentence, and seeing where it leads. I have started at the beginning of the story and told the tale chronologically. I have started in the middle and used flashbacks. I have written in both third person and first person narratives. I have no one method, no one way of approaching a story.

I have written novels based on the lives of prominent Cherokee figures from the past: Henry Starr, Ned Christie, Zeke Proctor, Captain Dutch, Dragging Canoe, and Sequoyah. With these, I had their history as an outline. Even so, one has many choices to make in writing such a tale: where to start, where to end, how to fill in the gaps that have been lost in history, how to characterize historical figures, how to determine motivation and create at least believable dialogueue, and most important of all, I think, write a novel as true to the facts as we know them as it is possible to write.

In approaching such a work, I first of all try to find everything that is available in print on the subject and read it. Where there are contradictions, I study them and try to discover the one version that makes the most sense to me. For example, when I was working on *Sequoyah*, I read in a couple of sources that he had twenty children and five wives. I could not find any evidence of that anywhere else. When Sequoyah died, his wife, Sally, received a pension from the Cherokee Nation, and the paperwork indicated he had only one son and one daughter, both of whom are mentioned in a variety of sources. I struggled with what to do about this dilemma until I finally came across the original source of this wild bit of information. It came from Sequoyah himself in an interview conducted by a man named Lorenzo Knapp while Sequoyah was in Washington D.C. as a member of a delegation from the Arkansas Cherokees. Sequoyah, who had to have been speaking through an interpreter, told Knapp that he had five wives and twenty children.

But Sequoyah told Knapp some other interesting things. He said that he had gotten the idea for his Cherokee syllabary by listening to the sounds of birds and animals in the woods, a perfectly silly idea. It occurred to me then that Sequoyah was simply pulling Knapp's leg. He had been in Washington too long and wanted to go home. He was growing weary of being interviewed and treated as a celebrity. He was tired of white men's foolish questions, so he gave foolish answers. He began telling Knapp things that he thought Knapp wanted to hear, and I'm sure he enjoyed the joke very much. It's a fine example of Indian humor at work. I wrote my novel accordingly.

Another problem from *Sequoyah* might be interesting if not instructive. Writers have disagreed with one another since Sequoyah's lifetime on the identity of his father. Was it Nathaniel Gist (or Guess), an Englishman? Was it George Gist, a German? Or some full-blood Cherokee whose name was never recorded? How would I deal with that issue? My answer came as a Cherokee. Traditionally, a Cherokee's father is simply not all that important. A Cherokee was born into his mother's clan. He had as many "mothers" as his mother and his mother's sisters all added together. He had as many "fathers" as his mother had brothers. His biological father spent more time with his own clan relatives than he did at his wife's house. A Cherokee woman could divorce her husband by tossing his personal belongings out the door. So, how did I deal with the problem of Sequoyah's father? By not answering it, by having Sequoyah shrug off the question as if it was of no importance.

Each historical novel produces questions like these that somehow must be answered by the writer. The writer must weigh all the available evidence carefully. If he is dealing with a culture other than his own, he should try his best to figure out that culture's attitude to that particular issue. Then, all he can do is his best.

There are other kinds of questions that come up as well. I remember writing something some years ago where I had a man in the 1800s in a store about to buy something. It was on the counter and he was ready to pay for it. I stopped writing. I asked myself: How much did that thing cost in those days? I stood up and stomped around the room for a while. I went to my library and pulled out any number of books in search of the answer. I don't recall how much time I wasted on that question before I came up with a very simple solution. I wrote something like, "He threw his money on the counter and paid for it." We don't always have to know all the details.

Smart writers also make use of their friends. I was writing a contemporary novel one time and I needed some information about a private airplane. I had a friend who was a pilot, and he happily told me everything I needed to know on the subject. I once asked a friend from Alcoholics Anonymous how to get someone off booze. He provided valuable help. Another friend who is both a writer and a medical doctor has called me for help on Cherokee cultural matters, and I have called him regarding how to deal with certain wounds back in the old days. I have a number of full-blood Cherokee friends on whom I rely heavily when dealing with sensitive matters when I am writing Cherokee material.

On a number of occasions I am asked to give advice to aspiring writers. My advice is always first to read, read, read. I firmly believe that the best way to learn to write is to read good writing. I have always been a reader. My mother taught me to read before I went to the first grade and she put me in school when I was five years old. I was reading Shakespeare at the age of ten. I never took a writing course of any kind beyond the required freshman composition in college. When we read good writing, we absorb, by a kind of osmosis, all of the grammar, the spelling, the punctuation, the style, the overall structure, in short, all of the things that make good writing.

I think I even found proof of this when I was teaching English in college. I cannot remember ever not being a good speller. When I was in junior high school, I could spell just about any word in the English language. Then, as a college English teacher, I read hundreds of English papers, most of them filled with misspelled words, and one day found myself not being able to spell some rather common words. Just as I absorbed the proper spelling of words from reading, I was now absorbing the misspelling of words from reading poorly written papers.

People ask me where my ideas come from. They can come from anywhere. Some years ago I was telling my wife stories about some of the crazier college professors I had known or heard about during my years as a student and then as a professor myself. "Write a book," she said. So I wrote *The Meade Solution*, a story about a group of graduate students in an imaginary college who are facing a bleak job market. One of them gets the idea that the old dusty professors are so eccentric that almost anything could happen to them and no one would be suspicious.

So he begins by systematically eliminating professors by taking clever advantage of their particular eccentricities until he has created enough job openings for himself and his friends. The book was published by the University Press of Colorado.

We often hear writers or teachers of writing tell us to write about what we know, or to write from experience. That's well and good, but I think it can be misleading. Students have told me they haven't lived long enough or haven't had any interesting experiences, and therefore have nothing to write about. If one is going to advise aspiring writers to write about what they know, for God's sake add, "And if you don't know it, there is such a thing as research." Or just reading. Anything we read is added to our experience. I read a book years ago called *Recollections and Reflections of a Japanese Artist*. I don't remember the artist's name, but he said that when we read the work of even long dead writers, we make friends with them. In that sense, Shakespeare must be one of my best friends. And General Lew Wallace, I think, had never visited the ancient Roman Empire when he sat in the governor's office in New Mexico and wrote *Ben Hur*, allowing other folks to worry about trivial political matters.

They tell us to write with a purpose. Sometimes I think that purpose may be nothing beyond entertainment. Some good novels don't do a damn thing beyond entertaining, and I don't see anything wrong with that if they do it well. Most of our lives these days require some kind of escape sometime, and I would rather see escape accomplished with a good book than with most other possibilities. But many, if not most, good novels go at least a little bit beyond that. They teach something. Even the simplest of western novels, for instance, usually teach something about morality, something about standing up for what one believes in, something about fighting for what is right, something about helping someone who is in need of help.

Beyond that, a good historical novel can often teach history better than a history book, a history course, or even some history teachers. But a novel can be, should be, sneaky about teaching. If it's done well, the reader should finish the book and say, "That was a good book. I really enjoyed it, but, by golly, I think I learned something along the way." A novel can be entertaining and educational at the same time. And that should be the goal of any writer of historical fiction and most writers of any kind. A writer who uses historical fiction to purposely distort the truth to serve some devious purpose is in my mind as evil as any murderer. So, I write with a purpose, and that purpose is first of all to entertain, and second, to educate.

Then they tell us to write for a particular audience. Just exactly who is this book aimed at? Well, I am here to tell you that I have never let that question interfere with my writing. I do not write for a targeted group of people. Ideally, I would like for everyone to read my books. I was reading Shakespeare at age ten, and I don't think Shakespeare was written specifically for me. Neither was Tolstoy or Pushkin or Dostoyevsky or Sophocles, but I have read them all. I write for anybody and everybody, and I write for posterity. I want my writing to survive.

I have been asked if I write for a Cherokee audience. I do not. However, I have said that if some powerful spirit appeared to me and told me, "I'll give you a choice. Your books will be read and appreciated by large numbers of Cherokee people, but you'll never make much money, or they will be widely read and you will get rich, but you'll be largely ignored by Cherokee readers," my choice would clearly be that I would take the Cherokee readers. Happily I do not have to make that choice. I have loyal readers from various walks of life. I am especially proud to add that included in that readership are a number of Cherokees who never read a book in their entire lives until they got hold of one of mine.

Another thing I've heard over the years is that an aspiring writer should work to develop his own style. That, I believe, is utter nonsense. I believe that one should work to develop a good writing style, unless it just comes naturally, and if there is such a thing as a personal style, it will just appear. I have no idea what my style is like as opposed to that of any other writer. I just write the best I can.

There is something very mysterious about the writing process, no matter how much one might plan, outline, or make meticulous notes before beginning a project. I can remember, as a college student, being in a Shakespeare class. After all the detailed explanation by the professor of a particular passage, a student would ask, "Professor, did Shakespeare know that he was putting all that in there?" I would think, "Of course, you fool. It's there and the pattern is perfect." Later, after I had written my first novel, I had an editor point out to me certain things he particularly liked about it. I was surprised. I had not known these marvelous things were even in there. I've had that experience over and over again. I've had to revise my response to that student I thought was stupid. Perhaps Shakespeare did not know that all that was in there.

Something happens in the writing process that we cannot explain. That's why the ancient Greeks came up with the concept of the Muse. That's why Dante said that God dictated to him. Yeats claimed that he engaged in automatic writing. Some writers say they have a spirit guide. Some will tell us that they just create characters and then follow them around. One writer once said that he had a whole bunch of characters running around on top of his desk, and he didn't have room for all of them in the novel he was writing. He begged about half of them to get out, but they wouldn't budge. At last, he said, he promised them that if they would get out of the way, he would write another novel just for them. So they left, he finished his novel, and then he wrote another making use of those characters who had so politely stepped aside.

Most of these people, if we took them seriously, would be put away in mental institutions. The idea of the Muse is every bit as crazy as is the notion of dozens of little men and women running around on top of a writer's desk. Where did these ideas come from? Why do writers say such things? It is purely and simply because of that mysterious thing that happens when one is writing. They are all various attempts at putting into words what cannot be put into words. There is some mysterious quality that is at work when we are writing. Personally, I do not understand it, but I will not tell you that I have a Muse, a spirit guide, or ghostly characters I am following, or little people running around in front of me on my desk. I just accept the mystery. We are not supposed to know all things.

Now let me consider some common misconceptions, or at least I consider them to be so. I have had people ask me what I do to overcome writer's block. My response is always that I do not believe in it. If I am a professional writer, then writing is my job. I once worked in a hardware store. I could not get up in the morning and say I had hardware store block and I'm not going to work. I do not get writer's block. I do have lazy days. I think any writer who claims to be suffering from writer's block is just having a lazy day and is using a common misconception as a convenient excuse.

It's like saying, I have to be in a cabin in the Rocky Mountains to write, or I have to be in Paris to write. That's really saying, I want to be in a cabin in the Rockies or I want to be in Paris and I'm going to use my writing as an excuse to get there. If one can write, then one can write anywhere. I knew a woman who wrote mysteries who told me that when she and her husband had only a small apartment, she used to put her portable typewriter on the toilet seat and sit on the floor to write.

Writers are like anyone else. They make up excuses for things they want to do or not do. I put off writing my novel *Mountain Windsong* for a few years because I said that I had to go to North Carolina to write it. At last I could put it off no longer. I wrote it in Iowa without ever having been to North Carolina. The opening scene was set in Big Cove, a community on the Cherokee reservation in North Carolina. A few years later I was invited to the town for a book signing and a reading. I read some passages from *Mountain Windsong* to a group of Cherokees. A lady in the audience asked my wife when I had been to Big Cove, and she replied never, that this was our first visit to the state. The woman practically accused my wife of lying to her. She said that I had to have been there to be able to write so realistically about it. This is first of all a lesson in research. Next, it's an illustration of how a writer can make excuses that might sound good to others in order to put off doing something.

It's also true, though, that being someplace can be a tremendous motivation for writing. Or being away from some place. My first job out of graduate school was in DeKalb, Illinois, and I hated the school where I was teaching. I found myself more and more thinking of Oklahoma. Because I am a romantic, I suppose, I thought about it mostly in the past. I thought about the stories my grandfather told about Indian Territory days before Oklahoma statehood. I began reading about those days, and then I began writing about them. Writing myself back home, I called it.

Some time later, after a nine year absence from Tahlequah, Oklahoma, we returned. My next few novels would never have been written if I had been anywhere else in the world. I found I could drive the streets of Tahlequah, the original capitol of the Cherokee Nation, and look at locations where historical events had taken place. I wrote three novels about a fictional full-blood Cherokee district sheriff in Tahlequah in 1873. I could locate his house exactly and pinpoint where the events I was imagining had taken place.

I love being in Tahlequah. I love going to the old capitol building downtown and imagining the chiefs and the council members I have read about actually being there 150 years ago. I can visualize the square before the two-story brick building was erected. It had a huge arbor for gatherings and two small log cabins on what is now the back of the square called Water Street. It follows the line of the creek, now called the Town Branch that was originally called Wolf Creek. The creek and the road both go all the way out to another community called Park Hill. Park Hill is where Chief John Ross and other prominent Cherokees of the old days had their homes, and I can see in my mind's eye Chief Ross being driven to work in a buggy by a black slave, right down Water Street to the capitol square. There are so many people who live in and around Tahlequah with no idea of the history surrounding them, but those of us who do remember the history live in a wonderland of ghosts and swirling historical episodes.

Remember that history is not just fun, it's important. Too many people these days think that anything that happened before they were born is ancient history, and further, and worse, they feel like they don't need to know anything about it, that it's unimportant. I believe it is important to remember the history, or learn it. I think it's also important to realize that it was not really all that long ago.

My own grandmother, to whom I was very close, was born in 1890, the year Sitting Bull was killed. She was born in the Cherokee Nation in Indian Territory. Oklahoma did not exist at the time. I have two separate snapshots with me, my father, my grandfather, and my great-grandfather, four generations in one snapshot. One more photograph, if such were possible, of the previous four generations would take me back to the American Revolution. None of that was that long ago, and that, I believe, is important for a writer to realize.

If we are writing historical fiction, or anything at all about the past, we are not all that much removed from it. It happened, we might say, just yesterday. The people were very real people. The things that happened are not just the stuff of dry history books. They are very real events that happened to real people, and we need to be aware of that fact. As writers, we also need to have a strong desire for others to have that awareness and to share that sense of the reality of history and of its nearness to our own lives.

I realize I have not been saying much about the writing process, how to write, and how I write. I have read things and heard writers talk about how to plot a story. I have never used any of it. Things just happen, one after another, and that is the story. I have read and heard about how to create realistic characters, and none of it makes any sense to me.

When I'm working on a story, I have mental images of the characters involved in that story. I can see them, I can hear them talk, and I can usually read their minds. That's one of the things a writer has in common with an actor. He has to be able to get into the mind of just about anyone: noble persons, creepy and degenerate killers, and others. How else can the actor portray them realistically? How else can the writer describe them so his readers will believe they are real people?

I wrote a novel once called *Brass*. It was based on a Cherokee mythological tale which dealt with a character who was a shape changer and a passionate gambler. At the end of the original tale, Brass is pinned to the ocean floor by means of a long pole through the middle of his body. The tale ends with the statement, "Brass will be there until the end of the world because he cannot die." I began wondering what it might be like if he were somehow freed and unleashed on the modern world. He might be a dangerous monster, but he would also be like a small child. Nothing would be familiar to him. He had been placed on the ocean floor sometime before Columbus. Everything would be strange. All would be somehow frightening.

As I wrote the book, Brass became a very real person to me, a character with his good side and his bad side. He killed, but usually for a good reason, from a child's point of view, because he was frightened or because he wanted something badly, or because someone had angered him beyond control. Most children, if they were powerful enough, would kill for any of those reasons. I could hear Brass's voice. I could see him, picture his movements. I could also read his mind. So how did I create this character? I have no idea. Writing a novel, to me, is almost like watching a movie in my mind. I have to see it. Only then can I write it.

There are other kinds of writing. Writing nonfiction is, to me, a totally different process from writing fiction. I probably could write something about how I go about writing nonfiction, but I don't want to do that. The mystery is missing from the process. At least it is for me.

Writing nonfiction is work. I don't enjoy it. I'm not ever sure when I'm finished that I've done a good job with it. Every time I finish a work of nonfiction, I say I'll never do another one. I've made a liar out of myself more than once.

The process of writing poetry seems to me much more like that of writing fiction. I've written a poem on exactly the same subject as a novel I wrote, and in the poem I have told the same story as I did in the novel. Obviously, the poem is much shorter, thus the words have to carry more meaning. Each line has to imply much more than it says. Beyond that, I don't know what to say about poetry. I'm not even real sure what poetry is unless I use the definition I read in a creative writing text once: Poetry is writing in which the writer rather than the printer controls the right hand margin of the page. I do know there is much doggerel verse being written these days that I won't call poetry. I'm rather fond of Lord Byron myself. I don't write much poetry anymore, though, because of the same kind of feeling I get from writing nonfiction. I'm never sure if the results are really worthwhile, and I know some very fine poets with whom I am most reluctant to compare myself.

So for the most part I'll stick to writing fiction. I enjoy doing it, I think I can do it well, and I believe more people will read what I have written. I think I can teach a few people a few things about the history of this country, particularly as it relates to the Cherokees. That gives me a real sense of purpose with my work beyond just struggling to make a living at this most insane way of going about that necessary task. It gives me a sense of satisfaction, it gives me pleasure, it feeds my ego, and I sleep well.

I would like to add just one thing. Don't take anything I have written here too seriously. That's not to say that I've been lying. I have told the truth, but what is the truth for me on this subject, on the writing process and everything related to it, may not be the truth for any other writer. We all approach it differently, according to our own abilities, attitudes, whims, and individual personalities. Another writer will likely tell you something very different, a third something equally individual.

We are all individuals. We each have our own set of private dogma when it comes to writing. That is perhaps the value, certainly the interest, of this collection. ႏ

Researching and Writing the West

David Dary

David Dary, a native of Manhattan, Kansas, is the author of more than a dozen nonfiction books on the American West, as well as many articles and book reviews. He is emeritus professor of journalism at the University of Oklahoma where he headed what is now the Gaylord College of Journalism. He is a former president of the Western Writers of America, Inc., and Westerners International. Dary has received several awards for his writing including two Spur Awards from W.W.A. and two Wrangler Awards from the National Cowboy and Western Heritage Museum. He received his second Wrangler in 2005 for *The Oregon Trail* (Knopf). Before entering higher education in the late 1960s, Dary was with CBS and NBC News in Washington, D.C. He lives in Norman, Oklahoma.

David Dary
(Photo by Ned Hockman)

I am a nonfiction writer who writes about the history of the American West. One does not have to be a trained historian to write about history.

Unlike reading, writing, and arithmetic, history does not require formal instruction to be handed down from generation to generation. We have all listened with interest as parents or grandparents told stories of the past. From these stories, as in the epic tales of old, one must sort out fact from fiction to learn the true history because it is often embellished. History can also be the propaganda of victors.

What motivates someone to write about history varies from person to person. In my case, it was the stories heard as a boy from my maternal grandmother and some of her brothers and sisters who grew up during the fading years of the Old West. One grand-uncle knew W. F. "Buffalo Bill" Cody. After Carrie Nation and her hatchet brought prohibition to Kansas, he also procured whiskey for Cody whenever the showman visited his sister in my hometown of Manhattan, Kansas. My grand-uncle also told of train after train going east through town in late spring and summer transporting Texas longhorns from Kansas cattle towns to the eastern markets. My grandmother vividly described how when she was a young girl, Indians came to her home and sat on the ground outside the back door when her mother baked fresh bread. They never went away hungry.

As the years passed, my curiosity about frontier life was enhanced by stories found in a few books and in westerns, those B movies that were shown on Saturday afternoons at the State Theater. However, I wondered how the cowboys and outlaws could fire more than six shots from their six-shooters, and why the scenery in movies supposedly set in Kansas did not match the prairie and plains that I knew so well. It was then I began to question the truth of what I heard and saw about history.

My curiosity about the world beyond Kansas grew during high school and pushed me toward a career in broadcast journalism. After graduating from college, my work took me to Texas where I marveled at the pride Texans had in their history. But when I compared it to that of my home state of Kansas, Texas history paled. However, reading the books of Texan J. Frank Dobie, who made simple events and people come alive, caused me to wonder why no one had written Kansas history with the same honesty and simplicity. Most of the Kansas writers I had read were dull, and their histories seemed filled with the nondescript careers of politicians and ministers while ignoring the frontiersmen and pioneers who ranched, homesteaded, or built the first towns with churches and established other eastern institutions.

My interest in western history was interrupted when my career took me to CBS News in Washington, D.C. Covering the White House, Congress, and other governmental agencies opened my eyes to the inner workings of government and provided insights on the government's role in settling the West a century earlier. In addition, I learned a great deal more about writing from well-known newspapermen and broadcast journalists. When I moved into management at NBC News, there was no more time to read on the West. I began building my own research library of books and pamphlets related to Kansas and the West. I took advantage of several fine used bookstores in Washington that offered countless books on the West, many of them once owned by former congressmen, senators, and government officials from west of the Mississippi River.

When Ted Yates, a producer at NBC, decided to make the television documentary "The Journals of Lewis and Clark" in the mid-1960s, he asked me, the only other westerner in the Washington bureau, if I knew where he might be able to record the sound of prairie dogs. I did, and soon I was engrossed in the saga of the two famous explorers. Yates's desire to recreate scenes resulted in his finding a large private herd of buffalo in northeast Wyoming. After filming winter scenes of buffalo, he returned to Washington with a buffalo skull used in filming the documentary. He later gave it to me, and it now graces our stone fireplace.

The story of the buffalo caught my fancy and the Library of Congress made it possible to read with ease just about everything written on the animal and its history. Not finding a comprehensive book on the buffalo, I decided to write such a work. It took ten years before *The Buffalo Book* (Swallow: 1974) became a reality. Angus Cameron, who had been J. Frank Dobie's editor at Little Brown, wanted to publish the book at Knopf, but he wanted me to change the focus from the animal to the buffalo hunters. I refused. Still, we became friends, and he later admitted that my approach turned out better than what he had wanted.

When NBC wanted to transfer me to New York, I said no and chose instead to return to my native Kansas where my mother's health was not good and where our children could grow up in an atmosphere similar to what my wife and I experienced. Helping to build a television station in Topeka and then working for a year in politics left no doubt that if I was to have time to write, the ideal setting was the academic world where I could apply my professional experience in journalism and teaching and still have time to research, write, and publish for promotion and tenure. After all, academicians are expected to conduct research and publish.

During the next twenty years, and armed with a terminal master's degree, I climbed the ranks to full professor in the journalism school at the University of Kansas. For nearly a decade, I taught, researched, and wrote articles on Old West history for *Star* magazine, the Sunday supplement of the *Kansas City Star*. When an editor suggested I put my stories in a book, *True Tales of the Old-Time Plains* (Crown: 1979) was the result.

About then Angus Cameron at Knopf asked if I would be interested in doing a book on the culture of the cowboy. Having spent more than a decade collecting material on cowboys and the nineteenth-century cattle trade, I jumped at the opportunity. Two years later, *Cowboy Culture* (Knopf: 1981) was published and made something of a splash. The book established a pattern for how I approached future books by providing greater background and depth, digging deeper for facts and fresh stories, and spending more time than ever in writing, editing, and rewriting to shape the material. It became my goal to produce books that accurately chronicled history with much clarity through stories about the characters and the time covered. Since people make history, their stories are the backbones of the past.

Like most writers, I have a room for my word processor and a research library. A nonfiction writer of western history needs good reference books, a good dictionary, legal pads for making notes, maps of western states, and file space to hold photocopies of research material. Having a workspace that you control is essential to any writer of western history.

When do I write? Beginning writers often ask this question, perhaps believing there is some secret to successful writing. The secret is hard work. I have no set time to write but prefer to write early in the morning or during the evening, yet I can remember days when I wrote during late mornings and during afternoons.

More important than *when* a writer writes is research. Thorough research is critical in nonfiction writing about the West. Having built my own extensive research and reference library, I begin by checking my bibliographies for books and pamphlets dealing with my chosen subject. The *Harvard Guide to American History* is often helpful, as is Henry R. Wagner and Charles L. Camp's *The Plains and the Rockies, a Critical Bibliography of Exploration, Adventure, and Travel in the American West from 1800 to 1865.*

Locating primary source material about the subject is important. I look for first-hand accounts by participants whether it be journals, diaries, written recollections, or something in government documents. I avoid reading secondary source material until after I have located and read the first-hand accounts. I also search the Library of Congress Web site under the subject or person I am researching and often come across valuable source books. From these and others, I compile a list of primary sources. If I do not have the books in my own library, I look for them in the Western History Collections at the University of Oklahoma. Having a good university research library is always a plus.

Gradually I review the material, often taking notes or obtaining photocopies of the information I want, and my research file grows. Since most of my book narratives are told in chronological order, my research file is organized in that manner. This initial research provides a sense of how the book will be organized. The next step is to create a chapter-by-chapter outline. With the outline in hand, I create blank files on my word processor, one for each chapter. Then, as material comes to hand appropriate for one chapter or another, it is placed in the appropriate chapter file. This process takes many weeks, but gradually the raw material begins to shape the chapters and the book.

Sometimes it is necessary to travel to where the stories occurred or to visit the libraries of state historical societies for material, including illustrations. This gives the mind a break from writing, although the mind never really rests during these breaks. Sometimes if I have a problem finding the right words to describe a scene or have a problem developing a transition in a chapter, the break gives my mind the opportunity to solve the problem or problems.

Once I fully understand the material, the story, I begin to write. From the start, my goal is to produce a rough draft with notes at the end of each chapter. Gradually the book takes shape, but it is not uncommon to cut and paste material from one chapter to another, or to quit writing on one chapter and work on another to give the subconscious mind time to solve a writing or organizational problem.

Maintaining your writing style throughout the book is important. Many times I make major revisions in the first chapter or two after much of the manuscript is finished in order to maintain the style that develops in the later chapters. Sometimes it takes two or more chapters before the juices really flow and the passion for the material takes hold. Once I start writing it does not mean my research work is over. In writing, rewriting, and editing chapters, I often realize I am missing something. At that point I search for the missing element, sometimes having to contact a distant library to obtain photocopies of the necessary information or to obtain a book on inter-library loan.

Once the final draft of the whole manuscript is complete, I play the role of critical reader and with a pencil or pen make revisions to correct errors and to maintain good thought flow throughout. Once the revisions are made, I usually ask my wife to read the manuscript with an eye to clarity. If there is anything she does not understand, she underlines it and marks the page with an X in the corner. She is my clarity check. Changes are made, the manuscript is read one final time, and, if necessary, revised again. The manuscript is then sent to the editor for comments.

While the editor is reading the manuscript, I begin the process of selecting possible illustrations for the book. I usually have some photocopies of illustrations in hand obtained during my research. It is necessary, however, to go through the manuscript draft to identify all of the places where illustrations would be helpful to the reader. If I have not already located appropriate illustrations for these spots, I contact selected historical societies to see if they can provide them. If no illustrations are located, consideration is given to finding an artist to produce the desired art. If maps are needed to reinforce the text and provide additional clarity, they are sought, or I produce rough maps myself to show what is needed and hire a professional cartographer to produce the desired maps.

It is not unusual to take a year or longer to produce a finished draft, and then there may be another year of reading proofs, rechecking the facts, and working with the publisher's copy editor, publicity people, and others before the book is actually published. One learns the entire process through experience. The more books one writes, the better one understands the process and can anticipate its needs.

Anyone writing about the American West reads what other writers in the field produce. During my early years in higher education, I admired the books on western history by J. Frank Dobie, J. Evatts Haley, and academic historians Bernard De Voto, Walter Prescott Webb, Ray Billington, Joe Frantz, and Robert Athearn. They wrote to be read. They attracted readers and sold thousands of copies. Many of their books remain in print.

Not long after *Cowboy Culture* was published, Robert Athearn at the University of Colorado stopped me at a meeting of the Western History Association to say he very much enjoyed my book and added, "It was written for the masses. Too many professors are writing their books for friends. Keep it up." Athearn's comments came as no surprise because I had already spent more than a decade in higher education—journalism and not history—and observed the inner workings of it. An eighteenth-century saying by English author Samuel Johnson had already convinced me that time does not really change the human condition. Johnson had written, "Men are generally idle and ready to satisfy themselves, and intimidate the industry of others, by calling that impossible which is only difficult."

By then, I also learned the truth of another Johnson saying, "No man but·a blockhead ever wrote except for money." To make money from writing, one has to produce something people will buy to read. Athearn, Billington, Frantz, and a few other academic historians realized this but they also recognized the importance of writing for a broad audience outside the community of academic historians. They believed it was their responsibility as historians to share with the world the knowledge they had uncovered. They sought to help the public understand and appreciate history.

By the late 1980s and early 1990s, however, this was not the case. Higher education had changed. Too many institutions of higher learning were becoming businesses perpetuating the myth that a college degree was essential for success. Their goal was no longer to produce an educated person but a degreed individual. Too many college degrees were fraudulent documents, testifying to an education that never occurred.

From inside the hallowed halls of academia it was easy to understand why many academic historians did not write to be read, and why so many of them selected narrow or politically fashionable topics that were about as interesting as pet rocks. The reasons were clear. Too many history students were taught to conform to stilted ways, and many were taught that theory and methodology were the most important professional requirements. Little attention is given to clarity and communication. Common sense was ignored. Too many students were not taught to write well, but then too many of their degreed professors never learned to write well either.

William Craig Rice, associate editor of the *Harvard Review*, summed up the problem when he wrote in the autumn 1995 issue of the *Virginia Quarterly Review*, "The talent for writing for a broad audience is considered secondary at best, a mark of intellectual deficiency at worst by academic historians."

The academic historians who do not write to be read contributed to the public's dwindling understanding and appreciation of history. The public's appreciation for academic historians began to fade. Pulitzer Prize-winning biographer, David McCullough, speaking at the University of New Hampshire in the middle 1990s realized this and charged that we were becoming a nation of historical illiterates. He added, we are "losing our past, losing our story."

By then, university presses were publishing fewer books on the American West by academic historians and more by writers from other fields. This trend continued into the early years of the twenty-first century because too many books by academic historians were dull and did not sell. Even commercial publishers shied away from books written by academic historians. University presses and commercial publishers both sought to publish well-written books that readers would purchase.

So, what exactly is good history writing for which readers would spend money?

Good writing about history is also good storytelling. It requires fact and emotion, two essential ingredients in any good story whether fact or nonfiction.

There are two ways to understand something. One is through emotion, through sharing a common experience. The other is through intellect, a detached and individual experience. Thus, there are two paths to understanding—the emotional path and the logical path. Fiction writers prefer the emotional path, and nonfiction writers the logical path.

Unfortunately, too many academic historians will tell you that nonfiction writing about history is noncreative. This suggests the writer of history does not need to use imagination nor excite emotion in the reader. Those who believe this write dull history.

The best fiction and nonfiction writers use elements from both the emotional and the logical paths. If you examine the best writing, you will discover it usually falls somewhere between both paths. An analogy might be that good writing falls somewhere between mathematics and music.

Good writing also requires the use of simple words, not the long, obscure, or pretentious words many academic historians employ, either to sound academic, to impress their colleagues and students, or to hide their lack of knowledge and understanding of their subject. Successful writers use vigorous English, stress clarity and accuracy, use simple words, and generally produce sentences containing one thought.

Too many academic historians fail to take time to select interesting subjects, and then fail to take time to shape their books into interesting narratives that tell interesting stories. Too often, they ignore the need for clarity. The story is lost, buried in a mountain of facts that makes it impossible for the reader to grasp the story. Much of this factual material should be compressed into the notes at the end of the chapter or book and not placed in the text. The writer must write to be read.

Readers will pay attention to facts only when they are interesting. To be interesting, factual information must be touched with emotion.

In nonfiction writing, the writer must also arouse the reader's emotions about things not previously considered exciting by the reader. To do this, the nonfiction writer must mix facts, not just opinions, with imagination and emotion. The problem for the writer of history lies in combining these elements judiciously and effectively. This is when the writer must breathe life into facts and use fewer and simpler words to stress clarity. The writer must relate the facts with passion, and the passion must come from the writer who must have enthusiasm for the material. If the writer has no enthusiasm, the reader will sense it.

Some fiction writing friends of mine have often asked, "When are you going to tackle fiction?" I have given serious thought to fiction writing, but before I get around to trying it, I usually run across a forgotten true story in an old book or newspaper and realize there are countless other true stories just waiting to be unearthed. Why make up a story when the nonfiction well is not dry?

Still, I do not hesitate to use many devices employed by fiction writers in my nonfiction writing. Since my books contain true stories, I try to apply fictional techniques to help the thought flow and to create emotion. One basic fictional technique is to produce a clear beginning to a story that will arouse curiosity in the reader's mind. I like to take the reader by the hand and lead them into the story. Next, I strive to produce a coherent middle of the story that may arouse some suspense in the reader's mind and keep them riveted to the page. When the ending comes, I keep it as brief as possible and try to inspire the reader with satisfaction.

The organization of material in a chapter often begins with an opening summary to establish the tone and theme. Next is an example story or stories followed by more summary material followed by example stories and so on. It is a pattern similar to the quote-summary-quote-summary organizational approach to newspaper writing. My pattern, however, is not cast in stone because the material in hand often determines what it will be.

The components of good writing are certainly not limited to writing about the American West. They apply to all good writing, but for me writing about the West creates enthusiasm that soon becomes a passion not found in other subject matter. I suspect it reflects upon my heritage as a westerner, my love of the land—the prairie and plains and mountains and desert—and the wide range of people to be found there. Had I been born and raised in New York City and pursued writing, the hustle and bustle environment of skyscrapers and concrete would probably have induced the same enthusiasm in me for writing about the Big Apple.

Having been born and raised during the Depression in a small Kansas town on the edge of the Flint Hills, I often think of that place where in the spring the bluestem grasses lose their winter gray and brown and turn a deep, rich green, a color that will soon fade with the coming of the hot summer sun. The clean sweet smells carried on the gentle warm breeze blowing up from the Southwest carries a freshness that the nostrils have not sensed since the Indian summer days of fall. For me, the story of the land is as much a passion as the story of the Indians who first crossed the Flint Hills, moving from one river valley to another, or the first pioneers who came up the Kansas River from Westport seeking better land and a better life.

If you were born and raised somewhere in the West, you probably have similar memories of the region where you have roots. If you still want to write about your West and have dreams of being a successful published author, do not quit your day job unless you have plenty of money in the bank, sufficient Wal-Mart stock, and the time to pay your dues while learning to write. The truth is, only a handful of writers earn a respectable living from writing. Most other writers have jobs that enable them to pursue their dream. You may not have the patience to receive a stack of rejection letters from publishers. You may find writing too lonely a craft, or you may not realize how much work is involved in writing nonfiction books until you try it. But, as Mark Twain supposedly said, "Anyone can write. All of the words are in the dictionary."

Nevertheless, it takes a special passion to stick with writing, editing, and rewriting, and the financial rewards are generally slim. Back in the 1970s, I calculated that for the tremendous amount of time it took to research and write *The Buffalo Book*, I probably earned about seventy-five cents per hour. At the time, this was well below the minimum wage.

Regardless, if you are determined to write about some aspect of the West, first read as much as you can about the subject you wish to write about. Build your own research library. It will help you save time. Read everything published on the subject beginning with primary sources. You may find that there are too many published books on the topic. If you are lucky, however, and find very few publications, it may be a subject ripe for more research and a comprehensive book. Remember this, what you write must have universal appeal if it is to find a waiting market.

If you have never had a book published, do not try to get a contract with a publisher before you ever begin. First, you have no record as a published author and most publishers will not give you a contract. Second, you may decide later on to give up on the project. It is better to research and write your book and then seek a publisher. Even then, an interested publisher might not accept the manuscript unless you agree to make the changes they want. There are no guarantees that you will succeed.

The same goes for finding a literary agent. Truly professional agents will usually not agree to handle an unpublished author unless he or she is already a well-known personality with a name that will sell. But, after your first book is published, it is easier to get a professional agent to represent you.

Writing is work. Writing normally does not provide instant gratification, something too many Americans seek today. When you finish your first book, you should feel a great deal of personal satisfaction. Unless you can get your manuscript published, that may be all you will get, for the competition in this business is great. During 2004, there were more than one hundred seventy-five thousand books published in the United States alone, and publishers turned down countless other manuscripts. But, if your mind is set, you have a good job and plenty of time to write, try it. It will take time and a great deal of hard work.

As Samuel Johnson wrote in *Lives of the English Poets*, "What we hope ever to do with ease we may learn first to do with diligence." U

Instant Coffee

Max Evans

Max Evans was born in Ropes, Texas, and worked as a cowhand when he was eleven years old. Since that time he has been a rancher, soldier, painter, miner, actor, and writer. Evans has won two Spur Awards, two Western Heritage Association Awards, and in 1990 was the recipient of the Saddleman Award for Lifetime Achievement in the literature of the West. Two of his books, *The Rounders* and *The Hi Lo Country*, have been made into films, and Evans has written four others. The Western Writers of America recently voted Evans one of the top dozen writers of the West along with such authors as Jack London and Dorothy Johnson.

Max Evans
(Photo by Pat Evans)

Evans is the author of twenty-eight books and several novellas. When he was young his hobbies were calf roping and fishing. Today, they include reading classic novels and watching fine films.

What in the heck are we going to do about all of these people who call themselves writers? They do their books on e-mail, the internet, on rented and borrowed presses. It seems like there are more books on the topic "How to Publish Your Own Books" than there are hamburger flippers at McDonald's nationwide.

Instant writers are everywhere and nowhere at the same time.

These publishing zealots sell countless tickets to symposiums where they offer lectures, advice, and demonstrations on how to invent a book at dinner and have it published before sunset the next day. The instant writer can also become an instant editor and publisher.

Then, of course, we have writers of columns and criticism by the uncountable millions on such varied subjects as the environment, politics, gardening, diet, cooking, pornography, law, and gossip, as well as love, death, and taxes. Presently, there is no known method of workable birth control for this generation of instants. They are multiplying faster than a plague of locusts, the kind of invasion that hides the sun.

There are, unfortunately, very few original novels published in this cascade of self-indulgence. These rarities are probably equal in number to the few old established publishing houses still left. I heard from an often reliable source the other day that Congress slipped a bill through with the usual pork highway funds to make such a rare occurrence as originality against the law. The same source swears that the penalties for this heinous crime are extremely severe. I do not doubt this source, because the few eligible voters who do read demand serial romance, mystery, horror, how-to, and slightly altered diet and sci-fi books as constantly as they insist on the same preparation of their breakfast coffee.

The so-called publishing world is not all gloom; some of it is boom. Autobiographies of any type of celebrity, and books by celebrities about celebrities, are hot tickets. Almost any book written by or about an oft-mentioned politician flies off bookstore shelves as well. And beware of being even-handed—that will bring about a swift remaindering. The writer must lean far, far to the left, or far, far to the right. This ensures that either directional tilt will have half the population as potential purchasers.

Ghost writers are now in boom times, so much so that they are even hiring their own ghost writers. One must write with one eye closed. It is now, in the land of scribblers, a one-eyed world.

Out here in the vast Southwest with all of its brilliantly colored openness, numberless writers have gone to bed as white people and woken up as Indian writers. More individuals suddenly become Indians than the total population of the entire Navajo Nation. That's a bunch. The majority of them are Tony Hillerman wannabes, certain they would sell millions of books as Tony has. The trouble is, even if they had a few drops of Indian blood, they do not have a true Indian soul or the secret knowledge that goes with it.

These supposedly Indian books that are being shipped to bookstores and then back to the shredders have caused forests to disappear and long- and short-haul trucks to be worn out. To be at least slightly fair, I have to say that a few of these books are superbly written and are paying the way for all the fakes in both prestige and pesos. However, it will take many centuries for the forests and the ink supplies to return to the norm. We have no choice but to find a substitute for the oil depletion caused by the wasted consumption of the transporters. That, sadly, is as permanent as lost memories. Most discouraging of all, many of these speedo writers do not read or care about the world classics in literature, the books that have survived the filtering of time. The classics have survived simply because they are the best. In my long and often eventful life, I have never known or even observed a first-rate writer who had not been, for a sizeable length of time, an obsessed reader of the world's classics. No exceptions.

Maybe the speedo writers truly believe this kind of reading is a waste of time because they are imbued, inundated, and drowned in the dogma of marketing on television, newspapers, mailers, trade magazines, and even pre-movie commercials. Oh, they do read written invitations inviting them to symposiums and conferences for instant writers on subjects such as "How to Become Rich and Famous Best-Selling Authors in Three Days with Little Effort." I am inclined to believe that most of them learned to read by studying these endless invitations.

I've experienced forty-five years of being asked what advice I have for a beginning writer. My answer used to be "Read, read, read the best. Then write, write, and write some more, day after day, year after year." Now I simply say to non-readers, "Don't do it, don't become writers."

We must overcome the foolish and wasted gesture of encouraging these "instants." They must be discouraged and sprayed like summer flies. Help, hell! They must be brutally informed that they don't have the dedication, the reading, or enough plain life experiences to make a pencil-point dent on a real writer's butt. Tell them without hesitation to stop this cloning of one another and their written words by any and all means including outer space electronic repetition or any variation thereof. These would-be, wannabe, speedo, on the cheap writers must be slowed, blunted, before the pollution becomes so great it speeds up global warming with the same velocity they became instant writers. The fate of the world is dangling. There must be sharpedged filtering of these fakers now. Now, before it is too late.

Here is the caveat. The precious, priceless exceptions are those fated few who have stayed hooked. They have paid both the painful and joyful price of openly absorbing the works of the great and superior writers. They have then gone on creating even when their writing rooms are knee-deep in rejection slips or until they have actually sold a few stories or books to legitimate publishers or periodicals. To these sturdy and courageous few we must give time, energy, hope, and our personal sacrifices to help them find and be acknowledged for their own place among those who can respectfully be—Oh, Lordy, I can hardly bring myself to utter the words—a writer, a real writer. This last sentence might seem like false modesty to some, but I can assure you there are those who know this is not the case.

Long, long ago in a land far away, I lived with my wife, Pat, in the ancient art colony of Taos, New Mexico, where we were both striving, if not quite starving, artists. Hungry? Yes, sometimes. I had written vignettes all my life, tossing the paper in various fires and applying sundry outhouse uses for them, exactly what they deserved. However, as I studied oil painting with my mentor, the great pioneer Potawatomi Indian artist Woody Crumbo, I was beginning to sell and truly learning how to paint. A bright future sparkled way out there among the stars of the clear Taos night.

There was a drawback, of course. I couldn't stop writing little stories for a few dollars. As this creative infection on paper intensified, I caught myself doing fiction that would much later be called "magic realism." I only placed two or three of these in about that many years.

Finally, I published a collection of short stories in book form called *Southwest Wind*. Just before the release date of the book, I was in the tiny Sagebrush Inn lounge desperately trying to peddle a sixteen-by-twenty-inch nocturnal oil painting for our survival. I had felt confident going in since I had met accomplished and famous people in that enchanted cubicle such as Millicent Rogers (Standard Oil heiress and famed collector of Indian jewelry) and the indomitable Mabel Dodge Lujan, the controller/helper of such people as D. H. Lawrence and Georgia O'Keefe.

The little lounge continued its blessings for me. I was sharing a table with a jovial Texas oil man who was well-read and loved art. He had already agreed to buy my nocturnal for two hundred dollars. He had not paid for the painting yet, but was buying the beverages. A small miracle was occurring. Into each life a little dust must fall.

There was a young, husky man at the bar. After he had overheard the names Midland, Odessa, and Andrews, Texas, he, influenced by strong drink and prejudices, came over, placed his hands on the table and announced his dislike of all things Texan in a loud, stupid, and profane manner. I resented the intrusion on our survival and the insults to my new friend, a true Texas gentleman and savior. Since he had agreed to pay a princely sum for my painting, I was certain he not only flew with angels, but was their chosen flight instructor. I said something in defense of him I fail to recall.

The young man asked me to step outside. I agreed, moving swiftly ahead of him so he wouldn't have a chance to whack me from behind. I went outside, closed the door, and waited. Sure enough, he opened it and stepped out into the starry Taos night. At that moment I brought a fist up from my knees and amazingly connected with the point of his chin. He sprawled under the bright stars upon some good Taos gravel.

I went back inside, rejoined my most precious patron, collected two one hundred dollar bills and a nightcap of fine brandy. I gratefully wished this true gentleman of the entire universe years of good viewing and the gift of good fortune.

When I departed for our little adobe house next to the west mesa of Taos, the young intruder had vanished. All in all, I was a happy young artist. One might wonder what all this has to do with writing. Everything. The book was published. The very first words I ever read about my scribbling in my first book review said something like, "If you read this book at all, start at the end, read to the middle, then throw it in the trash." The review was published in the Sunday edition of the *Santa Fe New Mexican* and perused by almost everyone who could read in the northern half of New Mexico, the heart of my creative world. The review was written by the young man I had smacked on the chin in defense of my patron in the Sagebrush Inn lounge.

So, to those few scribblers who have survived the grueling process, please take this valuable advice seriously—Never, ever hit a critic. Offer to buy him or her a beverage, if you must, but keep your fists in your pockets. You see, this young man later became a book critic for the *St. Louis Post Dispatch*, which, in those long ago times, was a major American review outlet. He continued his onslaught of my books that followed. Then, nothing.

I always wished him the best: The best of hot coals to walk on; the best editors to constantly demean and re-ink his awkward words of cruelty; the best . . . ah, well, my best wishes are endless. I say this for the benefit of others because his critique of my first book was 90 percent correct. His only mistake was in percentages. The book should have been tossed after reading one-third instead of the generous one-half he suggested.

Nevertheless, I went on pigeon-tracking across paper with an old upright Underwood typewriter, as modern as I would ever get. I did a biography of the wonderful old outlaw/gambler Long John Dunn of Taos. Since there were many parts of his life I was asked by him not to write about, I was totally amazed that the biography got a lot of good reviews. Several New Mexico and Texas writers had wanted mightily to do his story, including his good friend Mabel Dodge Lujan. I was not aware at the time just how close he was to this grand and contradictory lady or I would have gone a little more epic. Even so, there were things that I couldn't tell about their relationship.

Then with my mentor, Woody Crumbo, I veered off for a spell painting, prospecting, and developing mines. We made a lot of money. We gave away a lot of money. We lost a lost of money when copper dropped from forty-eight cents a pound to twenty-four in less than 120 days. We went broke. Busted. In my case, I went $86,000 below nothing. That would be close to $400,000 in today's currency.

No money. No paintings. No art supplies left. Nothing. So, in great wisdom, I decided to write my first novel and pay off our debts that were growing daily. I will never know why Pat didn't up and leave me.

I wrote *The Rounders* because I knew the subject. I held nothing back in the book. I'd had my working cowboy days down in the manure-spiced dirt on the range and down in the whiskey gutters and jails while in town. That's the way it was in the postwar West. The novel got rejection slips from eleven major publishers, but my agent, Henry Volkening, who was from the old school, believed in it. He sold it to the Macmillan Company on the twelfth time out. To my eternal surprise, it got 99 percent good reviews and was optioned five times as a movie before Burt Kennedy talked Henry Fonda, Glenn Ford, and Chill Wills into starring in it, thereby getting the green light from MGM Studios. They didn't know exactly what category to put it in, so they tried to more-or-less throw it away. In spite of them, it hung on and became a hit in so many ways I cannot count them. It was also made into an ABC prime time television show starring John Wayne's son, Pat, and with Chill Wills repeating his Jim Ed Love role. The book has been in print for forty years. None of the above means as much to me and my family as paying off all those mining debts.

Once, when a stranger asked me what profession I was in, I choked and sputtered like an old 1920 Fordson tractor to attempt an answer without stating that word, "writer."

Then, my best friend from northeastern New Mexico, Wiley Hittson (Big Boy in the movie), got shot and killed by his younger brother. The terrible incident got my mind dwelling upon how I could fit it into a story of that vast, rolling grassland. I intended to write *The Hi Lo Country* novel with the killing of my friend as the driving force, yet subtly make the hugeness of the productive, lonesome land both hero and villain. In doing so I was certain I must reveal the people, the domesticated and wild animals, and the erratic weather as distinct and singular as the sun. I was also going to include a decimating drought, a bone-numbing, killing blizzard, and the endless wind to show the emotional and physical damage thereby wrought. To cap the milk bucket with cream, there would be a deadly love story with its own form of terrible beauty. Oh, I almost forgot—this must all be concentrated to an essence of perfectly balanced tragedy and comedy in no more than a 250-page manuscript. Nothing to it, I thought.

Then, there it was, I'd done it. I edited through with some elation, yet there was a strange uneasiness gnawing in the parts of my body that had been broken, or at least torn and badly bruised. That was most of me.

The rereading became more painful each time. I had gathered my original intentions in a tight bundle for sure, but somehow the pieces didn't quite mesh. I had about given up trying to solve the vexation; it was painful and discouraging. I was never going to earn the honor of using that distinguishing word, "writer."

Pat sat down with a pencil searching the script for hidden flaws. That day I saddled up our car and drove all the way to the ski lodge near our failed copper mines. No solace there. Since not a single word on the Hi Lo subject was spoken between Pat and me on the second day, I spent it in the Taos Inn consuming tasteful beverages with one cowboy, one miner, and one writer. We had some fun, I'm sure, in spite of the fact that I was preparing my entire being to return to painting full time if Pat didn't solve the Shakespearean-sized puzzle.

The third day she did it. I had two chapters completely out of sequence, and a third one she reworked extensively. To this day I don't know how I got the feeling, the rhythm, the honest vernacular of it so wrong. Pat put enormous effort into getting it right.

Since writers are not very smart, I finally saw the priceless work she had done. At last, with Pat's patient help I could see a book. I had been as close as the distance between a flea's eyes to forever and ever being a painter.

The big little novel was finished and for the first time I thought I had finally passed the scribbling stage. The fun had just started with the misadventures of the Hi Lo work. Most of it had been written about myself and others many times over, so we'll just state only that the great director Sam Peckinpah fell in love with it and struggled for almost a quarter of a century trying to get it made into a film. More than thirty years after Pat solved my problem with the book, Martin Scorsese propelled it into a film that we dearly love.

There must be a lesson here somewhere for some poor confused writer. I put my blood, my broken bones, hide, and soiled soul into this little book and with help, hung in there until it made its many strange moves. The options we sold were responsible for at least five of my later books being written and buying food for my family for many years. Is irony what a scribbler's world is all about? As I've already hinted, a writer's greatest asset is their being naturally doltish, so much so that attempting the impossible is often its own, and maybe their only, reward.

After deciding I had finally earned the right to be called a writer, I launched in and wrote three short novels released in a single cloth edition for Houghton Mifflin. They were *The One Eyed Sky, The Great Wedding,* and *My Pardner*, the one I enjoyed doing the most. The latter was optioned over and over by Sam Peckinpah for a film but he could never get a script. The Peckinpah estate owns the film rights, and Dave Peckinpah, Sam's nephew, and I are now doing a screenplay. All three of these short books were later published singularly in both cloth and paper versions. *The One Eyed Sky* got great reviews, but only sold two modest editions. No matter, I was ready to charge ahead, and I did.

At the beginning of the millennium, I felt that I might get one or two more books down on paper while in this dimension. So, I decided to read and reread some of the old and newer classics I had appreciated so much. At the same time I was scratching my own words into existence before it was too late.

Since I accidentally discovered Balzac's work on a ranch house bookshelf when I was about eleven years old, he has been my all-time most admired writer. First, he qualified by being more naïve than a one-eyed goat. He remained constantly in heavy debt even when he was selling more books than anyone in all of old-time Europe. The greatest love of his life was a Polish countess who he never even met until a year and a half or so had passed. He finally married her when he was too feeble to get out of his sickbed or even be carried on a stretcher to a true matrimonial bed. I really felt a kinship with him when I found that the little pot-bellied Frenchman had ridden across some big island on a jackass for many tortuous days to look at and purchase a dormant mine. He bought it and fruitlessly poured the next several years of royalties into the hole in the ground. He finally gave up on the endeavor and searched for other ways to dissipate the money he had made writing for about twenty hours a day. The mine was later developed by someone else who made millions.

Balzac's vision was always right but his application thereof was hopelessly in despair. He thought he could write anything and he did. Balzac could take his reader to a parlor or a party of the French aristocracy and you could see and feel the glazed patterns on the pottery as clearly as all the scheming for position, the bargaining for power and wealth, the pursuit of gluttony and lust, with a flow of intriguing, rhythmic words as revealing as a split watermelon.

Balzac could take his reader on a working, smelling, visual tour of down-in-the-dirt, potato-raising peasantry so thoroughly that thoughts of a hot shower followed after every reading. Just as in the Faustian novel *The Fatal Skin*, he leaped into the metaphysical world with a power that could move stone monuments. His scope and skill were unlimited. His personal existence was about 80 percent irresponsible. He wrote humor with the bawdiness of the peasantry and satire of the aristocracy so smoothly that the reader is mostly unaware of his astonishing range. Oh, how I enjoyed rereading forty-four of his works, some of them for the third time.

In between my own word-pushing, I took on Somerset Maugham's entire shorter works. I had remembered in my youth how he was in my favor, while the world's critics, both commercial and academic, were finding fault with his rather astonishing output. To hell and more to them. He was smoother and more insightful in skillfully and carefully constructed stories than the critics allowed. Maugham was simply a superb storyteller. Thank you, sir, for your clear revelations of the human beast and its varied environments.

I couldn't get to all these stories while attempting to finish my own life's work, but I did read Homer's *Odyssey* and Tolstoy's *War and Peace* (for the third time). To my surprise, *War and Peace* was even more amazing with each reading. How was it possible for anyone to show an army scattered over two or three thousand miles and make the reader actually see the private's squalid battlefield existence, as well as the general's occasional luxury of power, fears, and moments of brilliant tactics mixed with days and years of tragic mistakes? He also showed, as Balzac did, how the privileged, and their chattel peasantry, across the vast lands were existing, loving, and plotting. The latter maneuvering every bit as skillfully and as deranged as the plots of the privates were to their generals. Tolstoy is a writer to honor.

Then, on to the New Testament. While marveling at some of the strangely paced presentations and dialogues of great beauty, there is still some confusion in the awesome words. How could dozens of writers, over approximately two hundred years, construct the best-selling book of all time and expect it to be none other than the world's first and still greatest mystery. As has been constantly proven in my surprisingly long life, I am far too dense to even attempt an answer.

Anyway, the rereading of the Bible, along with Shakespeare's col-lected works, was a waste of quickly dissolving time for Ol' Max. They were written to be quoted aloud to appreciative audiences. I lack the brain power to remember a single line to quote, a failing I have strug-gled with most of my life.

In this rereading of what I remembered as the best, Homer's *Odyssey* alone diminished slightly to me. Who couldn't accomplish all of those daring deeds if he had the gods of the sun, stars, and oceans to learn from and be fortified by? Beautifully told, but not many accomplish-ments for Ulysses considering all the backing he had. I appreciated the old goat herder who took him in near the end of the epic far more than all the rest of the cast with boundless galactic magic supporting them.

So, for a spell I became even more culturally incorrect. I moved from reading dead white men's writings to reading dead white women's writings. They were of a more recent vintage and one still lived almost through my reading of her. That was Eudora Welty.

First, I went through the collected works of Colette, one of my favorites. I made a lovely discovery by pure accident: There will always be a single line or short paragraph in her wonderful writing where lightning strikes the observant reader. It is tremendously illuminating in the power and vision the reader receives for the rest of her story.

Then there was Katherine Anne Porter, Welty's mentor. I personally feel this wild and foolish creature is one of the world's most overlooked writers. Maybe she is still getting her overdue appreciation in her native Texas and a few other places, but like Maugham, I haven't heard or read any of our so-called contemporary intellectual leaders whispering her name, much less singing her praises.

In my recent rereading madness, Steinbeck's short novels and short stories balanced tragi-comedy better than just about any American writer. Gabriel García Márquez seems just as magical as his subjects. And then there are those who are writing well about the West and are far too numerous to mention. A few shoot-em-ups are still printed and appreciated, but the sci-fi invasion on television and movies, along with electronic games and media, have enslaved the minds of the young as B westerns once did to my generation.

The publishers will go with what the public will buy and the agents go with what the publishers will buy and the writers go with what they think the agent can sell. It's all locked up like an underground safe. The true dumb-asses like me will gamble a big chunk of their lives doing something original. However, we do have a few writers who are very skilled at historical westerns, and the publishers can actually sell their books. There have been so many who have been able to make this transformation that I hesitate to even try naming them, but a few who wham into my mushy brain are Elmer Kelton and his Texas Ranger books, J. P. S. Brown's Sierra Madre works, Richard S. Wheeler's gold and silver mining days, Bill Gulick's passionate telling in novel form the history of the great Pacific Northwest, Dale L. Walker's original adventuring with his *Pacific Destiny*, Win Blevins's *Stone Song* and his historical novels of mountain men, and Robert J. Conley's wonderful renditions of his Cherokee kin in the *Real People* saga stands alone. And then there is that one-in-a-zillion occurrence such as Rudolfo Anaya's *Bless Me, Ultima*. This first time through the ropes became an instant classic and has remained so for decades. There are so many fine historical novels that one has hope for another kind of freer future for original fiction.

The list might begin with a writer of the West, Margaret Coel. She has transcended the serious obsession with pure talent. There are a few others who have also accomplished this seemingly impossible feat. Dr. David Stuart's *Guaymas Chronicles* is a true story so good it could rank with literary fiction. However, we must add to the short list of true literary nonfiction Truman Capote's *In Cold Blood* and Norman Mailer's *The Executioner's Song*. There are such beginning novelists of contemporary western fiction as Sharon Niederman (*Return to Abo*) and Slim Randles (*Sun Dog Days*). They make the old pulse pound with expectation.

Right now, writing the West the best are women. They have an inborn ability to see details of truth that often amaze me. I am, as I've often proven, foolish enough to predict that over the next forty years a large number of the pioneering methods of telling our endless and individual stories of the West will be signed by women.

Elmer Kelton, J. P. S. Brown, myself, and less than a measuring cup of others, occasionally write of our post–World War II West in all its forms right up to date. Maybe I'm the only one senseless enough to keep trying to write the contemporary West in near totality. On an even smaller scale, as I do, writing about the modern Southwest is like successfully ramming your head through endless brick walls only to find that the last wall is built against a solid rock mountain. All one can say is, "Ouch."

Every now and then, when I can gather the courage to attend a writers' gathering, I suggest that there is a very wide opportunity for some blindly courageous person to bring off a *Gone With the Wind* of the West. Instantly there is a chorus from other authors that it has already been tried and failed financially, so the publishers have no interest. During my little jaunt through this society, I've witnessed scores of people trying to write like people from Hemingway to Louis L'Amour. Regardless of the vast differences here, they both achieved fame, one just as successfully as the other with almost totally different readers and type of books. Somewhere there is a man, a woman, or a child reading the best who will someday lay their ears back, grind their teeth in agonizing symphonies, and do the damn deed.

I revealed, with my *Bluefeather Fellini* book, the final proof of the mathematical madness of the word "writer." All the time I was wonderfully misspending my youth in Taos, I was making notes for a book I someday hoped to do. I didn't know what the heck it was going to be, but in my mind I called it "The Book of the Southwest." I had no plot, only an unrelenting itch. I still have the notes, scores of them, written down on bar napkins from around the country, mining stationery from the early and middle fifties, and such odd pieces of paper as hardware and grocery store shopping bags.

Then, over thirty years later, when I was sixty-seven years old, there came a day when I had to go through the notes and decide whether to do the book or not. The notes were all brief, some symbolic. Suddenly I realized there was enough material on those odd pieces of paper for twenty books. So, I took a walk of mental and spiritual turmoil in my backyard. Considering the wars, wrecks of all kinds, and often the careless lifestyle I'd lived, I figured the odds were against my finishing twenty books in this dimension. Suddenly a clear vision came to me: I would concentrate the twenty books into one, and I would title it Bluefeather after my totem, the mountain bluebird, and Fellini after Federico Fellini, my favorite film director at the time. I would do it if it killed me, and it damn near did. Five-and-a-half years later, in my seventies by then, the eleven hundred-page manuscript was complete. I knew it was *the* work of my lifetime.

It was praised highly by several editors who admitted they had no idea how to handle such a strange work. Greg Tobin at Bantam said he'd be happy to publish the paperback version if I could get a cloth edition sold first. My agent had sent *The Rounders* out eleven times with almost the same reaction years earlier. I decided not to risk all that time I might not have. Luther Wilson, director of the University Press of Colorado at the time, had already read and understood what the book truly was about. The press had never published a piece of fiction, a real challenge to Luther. It took enormous courage for him to convince the committee on something so oddly original.

Pat painted a beautiful blue feather arrangement for the jacket and Luther published it in cloth. To our surprise, it went through three editions with very good, if sometimes hesitant, reviews. The Quality Paperback Book Club picked it up, featured it in their catalog, and we sold three more editions. Surprisingly, the press and the book got a big write-up in the *Wall Street Journal*. Then, it went into mass paperback. Nothing really big here, I suppose, but after thirty-six years I had seen what I had been after all my life, without being totally aware of it, come to fruition. It was, after all, a book of the Southwest. It had all the nationalities and cultures that I had been so deeply involved in. It had the prospectors, the spirits, the animals, the earth and all of its rooted elements, the empire-builders, love and war, fun, and many different forms of tragi-comedy. So, there you have it—a highly foolish, even dumb attempt at something widely original, with uncountable years of odds against it. But it worked.

I slowly gained back my faded strength and have produced short stories, novels, essays, my one and only historical fiction novel, *Faraway Blue*, the text portion of two photographic books, a biography, *Madam Millie*, and at this chicken scratching I have three books down in first draft. I will be 1,019-years-old on my next birthday and still brainless enough to try to finish editing the three unfinished tomes and maybe even get a movie made of my little book, *Xavier's Folly*. Everything is destiny or nothing is destiny. Which is it? With that thought, I must prepare to end this essay. Or does anything ever really end? Or is it all beginnings, again and again?

In March of 2005, I checked out the *New York Times* and *Publishers Weekly* best-seller lists since they are the two most quoted. They both give the top fifteen best-sellers in fiction and nonfiction. *Publishers Weekly* does this for both cloth and paper. Sure enough, there were still a few political and celebrity books on the lists. I deliberately chose the time periods of the national election, and then Christmas, to observe the trends. Politicians and celebrities obviously sell the most during these two time slots.

For the fallow period of these categories, I decided to use the weekly best-seller list of America's number one daily newspaper, *USA Today*. They list the top fifty books in a row. It is all-inclusive, with fiction, nonfiction, how-to, and all kinds of other books listed, including mass market paperbacks. On Thursday, March 3, 2005, the prices ranged from $6.95 to $12.95 for trade editions on up to $27.95 for the most expensive cloth brand. Here's how the best-sellers broke down by category: How-to (11), romance (10), mystery (9), diet (4), suspense (2), biography (1), expose (3), and in the category of remotely possible literary works there were three novels. Right beside this list there is a weekly column called "Beyond the Top 50." It listed eleven health and diet books. Out of these sixty-one books there were the three novels already mentioned and not a single book featuring the West. That is, of course, no longer surprising. However, it makes one wonder how such a vast, adventurous, and productive chunk of the world has been so summarily dismissed. I'd like to know why. I would hope that someday at least one of the elite critics and purveyors of writing lore will give us the reasons for the above with honesty and a little dignity as well.

The *USA Today* best-seller list only emphasizes that we get diet books and other series mostly by the same authors year after year, just like cereal and soap boxes labeled "New and Improved." We are getting the secrets of life on the installment plan.

Well, both you cowards and courageous ones have gained a small glimmering in the mighty mystery of the universe and the simple truth about writing to charge forward or run backwards. I prayerfully hope for the latter. Oh, a couple of last thoughts should be strained from this gravel-filled skull. Please totally disregard the so-called intellectuals. These creatures are so wrapped up in their own little cocoons they are almost totally unaware of what makes the clay and blossoms of the world. If they were not so sure of their superiority they might dumb down enough to produce more than an average of two or three real writers per decade.

We now live in a world of serials. With serial movies and serial books on the universe, why be surprised at the plethora of serial killers and rapists, serial sci-fi, fantasy, horror, detectives, cops, corpse examiners, dog and cat and monkey doctors, and serials on television. There are spin-off serials and spin-offs of spin-offs, ad infinitum. Serials are growing with the increase in population. How could a small original book ever be found by a reader in this great morass. AND NOW ANNOUNCING . . . the comedic comic book! The unfunny publications that through dominant cartoon and semi-realistic drawings cut a person's terrible struggle to write—or read—down to almost nothing. Glory in the great best-sellers, movie and university teaching to come from these.

Do not concern yourself about how little notice or financial returns you get from your gut-written words, and don't be jealous of your more fortunate serial-writing peers. It will damage your work and your life. Do not allow it. Those rich and famous people you hear about almost daily will be culled down to a very, very minute number in fifty years, and most of us will be blown out of sight and mind by the ceaseless Southwest wind. No matter what, struggle on in originality. Your chances of surviving the unrevealing test of great-grandfather time are as good as the next scribe. ∪

Six Great Editors
I Have Known

Bill Gulick

For many years a regular contributor to *Liberty, Saturday Evening Post, Esquire,* and *Colliers,* Gulick has written two hundred stories, newspaper, and magazine articles, television scripts, screenplays, and dramas for the stage. Several of his twenty-seven novels have been turned into movies, including *Bend of the River, Road to Denver,* and *Hallelujah Trail.*

Gulick's first nonfiction book, *Snake River Country,* now in its fifth printing, won the Pacific Northwest Booksellers Award as the best nonfiction book of the year. He has written eight nonfiction books, all of them still in print.

Making his home in Walla Walla, Washington, for the past fifty years, most of Gulick's writings have been about the Pacific Northwest. His late wife, Jeanne, assisted him in research, secretarial, and editing work in her position as Northwest Librarian

Bill Gulick
(Photo by John Froschaur)

at Whitman College, where most of the material they gathered is now deposited. For many years, he has worked with the Nez Percé, Umatilla,

Walla Walla, Cayuse, and Yakima Indians on projects dealing with their land, water, fishing, and sovereignty rights.

In 1976 Gulick was project director for a twenty-four-thousand-dollar Washington State Humanities Commission grant given for the Outdoor Historical Drama he wrote and produced, *Trails West*, in conjunction with Whitman College and the Whitman Mission National Historic Site, and to pay Indian advisors and actors performing in the production which ran for 110 performances during the summers of 1976 and 1977.

In 1966 Gulick won the Western Heritage Award given by the National Cowboy Hall of Fame for his historical novel *They Came to a Valley*. In 1983 he was presented the Saddleman Award by the Western Writers of America for his impressive career writing fiction, nonfiction, and drama of the American West.

Addressing the Professional Writing School class I attended at the University of Oklahoma many years ago, Dr. Walter Stanley Vestal Campbell made a comment I never forgot. "You come to me saying, 'I know how to write. Teach me how to sell.' I say to you, 'You've got hold of the wrong end of the stick. If you apply yourself, I can teach you how to sell, but you'll be the rest of your life learning how to write.'"

Dr. Campbell was correct. By the end of the term I had sold my first story to *Peace Officer Magazine* in Oklahoma City for ten dollars. Sixty-four years later, I am still learning how to write.

My first story was published in September 1940. Since that time I have sold two hundred or more magazine stories and newspaper articles at slightly better rates, twenty-seven novels, eight nonfiction books, have made half a dozen sales to movies, and have written three plays done as outdoor dramas. Along the way, I have dealt with many editors whose quality has varied from incompetent to great. Looking back, I'll leave the bad ones to the anonymity they deserve and tell about my relations with the six really great ones I have known during my career, those who taught me what a writer needs to know.

FOSTER HARRIS

When Dr. Campbell established the Professional Writing School at the University of Oklahoma in the late 1930s, his colleagues in the English Department were so horrified that a member of their esteemed faculty would advocate writing for money that they kicked him out and into the School of Journalism. There, he was welcomed with open arms. A Rhodes Scholar, W.S., as his students and friends called him, was something of a maverick, for he had been raised on a Sioux reservation, was fluent in sign language and the Sioux tongue, had many Indian friends, and had published prestigious nonfiction books such as *Kit Carson, Sitting Bull, The Missouri River,* and *New Sources of Indian History,* even though he was not a degreed historian. As I came to realize during the twenty years he was my teacher, mentor, and friend, this made him a double pariah—to the English professors because he advocated writing for money, and to the history professors because his way of writing a book about the Little Bighorn battle was to bring a Sioux warrior who was in it to the O.U. campus, set him up in a tipi in his backyard, and interview him between classes instead of researching fifty weighty tomes written by experts in the field and then quoting them with proper credit.

While at Oxford, Harris had come to admire English ways to the extent that he accepted the Samuel Johnson dictum: "No man but a blockhead ever wrote except for money." Thus, he set up the Professional Writing School at O.U., his class accepting twenty would-be writers each semester who listened ten hours a week to W.S. talk about market requirements and the professional attitude, while his assistant, Foster Harris, a selling writer and an editor himself, gave each student a half-hour session once a week during which he read what the student had written, sliced it to pieces, and left it and the student's spirits bleeding on the floor.

"Bill, you've got a good opening for your story," he once told me. "Trouble is, it's over on page six. . . ."

So those first five-and-a-half beautiful, well-crafted pages I had worked so hard to create gave way to a sentence on page six which began, "Drawing his gun, he turned. . . ."

A man in his early forties, Foster Harris had been deafened by an explosion while serving in the National Guard, so he wore a hearing aid that he turned off when he did not want to listen to what was being said. He was an inveterate pipe-smoker, removing the pipe from his mouth only to eat, speak, or sleep. Like many editors in those days, he was a speed-reader, needing only two or three eye-fixes a page to absorb its contents, taking less than five minutes to read a twenty-page manuscript. By watching his pipe waggle as he read, I could tell whether he liked or disliked my story. If it moved back and forth horizontally, he disapproved. If it moved up and down, he liked it. In my case, I wrote a half-dozen stories before I got the up and down movement I yearned for.

Because I was working sixteen hours a day trying to become a selling writer, I literally dreamed stories. One night, I had a dream so vivid that when I woke up I immediately put it on paper. In the story, a veteran law officer awaits the arrival of a stagecoach carrying a man just released from prison after serving his time. An enemy of the ex-convict is also waiting, swearing to kill him, though the law officer's duty is to protect the man. The twist of the story is that the law officer still has a bullet in his chest that eventually may kill him, a bullet fired by the ex-con arriving on the stage. But he must do his duty.

After finishing the story, I took it to Harris and he read it, his pipe bobbing up and down from beginning to end. When he finished, he said, "You've got it, Bill. This one will sell."

And it did, for ten dollars to *Peace Officer Magazine,* whose editor offered me the bonus of getting me "into any jail in Oklahoma, including death row at the state prison, to research your future stories," which I never asked him to do.

"Inspiration" was not quite the word that Harris gave the students in his classes. Rather, it was "acceptance" as a professional, the standard W.S. had established for the courses he and Harris taught. In baseball, there is a great difference in playing the game for fun or for money. In writing, exercising one's linguistic skills to express oneself or to write stories for pay also requires crossing a wide river.

In some ways, Harris was a mystic, as I then interpreted the meaning of the word, for he often said things I did not quite understand such as: "The wheel has thirty spokes, yet its utility lies in the emptiness of the hub"; "Every ying has its yang", "Writing can't be taught, but it can be learned. If you're tough enough, I'll learn you"; "You've got to feel a story before you can make the reader believe it"; "Heroes are subjective; villains, objective."

By the latter, he explained, "The hero of the story always knows where he is going, though he has no idea of how he is going to get there. He is driving his pickup truck across roadless country without a map, but the farther he goes, the fewer obstacles he finds in his way. The villain, on the other hand, is facing backward in the bed of the pickup, counting fence posts, bumps, and telephone poles as they pass, so the further the pickup travels, the more fence posts, bumps, and telephone poles he writes down on his list, knowing only where he's been but without a clue as to where he is going."

As Ralph Waldo Emerson wrote over a hundred years earlier, "A hero feels and never reasons; and is therefore always right."

Harris's more serious students came to realize that he and his wife, Jill, were always home to aspiring writers, the coffee hot, cookies and snacks available. In return, when writers made a particularly big sale, we would rent a suite at the swankiest motel in town, buy some booze from the local bootlegger (Oklahoma was then a dry state), and throw a party with W.S., Harris, and Jill the honored guests. When invited, Jill would beam and exclaim, "A party? Oh, good! I'll bake a cake!" If you've never washed down a piece of Jill's chocolate cake with a glass of I. W. Harper's bootleg bourbon, you haven't lived.

Though I sold another ten-dollar story to *Peace Officer Magazine* without visiting death row, I wanted to move on to bigger things. Harris encouraged me to write a western for the Popular Publications chain that had thirty-three magazines on the newsstands each month, eight of them westerns.

"But I don't like shoot-em-ups," I complained. "The very idea of two men meeting to duel at high noon on a dusty street is ridiculous to me."

"Then write something else. Do you like horses?"

"I tolerate them in ROTC, as they do me."

"Any ideas for a horse story?"

"Well, a friend of mine who is really good with horses told me a story the other day about a horse he tamed, though nobody else in the class would go near it. What he did, he said. . . ."

"Don't tell it to me," said Harris, turning off his hearing aid. "Write it."

So I put a lonely teenage boy on a remote ranch with a pet stallion named Midnight, which has gone so crazy it tries to kill every person that comes near it. The boy's father says it must be destroyed, giving the boy a week to work with the crazed animal before he puts it down. Near the end of the week, the father is shot and gravely wounded by Indians, who destroy the corral and free all the horses except Midnight, who is stalled in the barn. The boy and his mother realize that only an operation can save the father's life, so a doctor must be fetched from town, ten miles away. The only horse available is the crazed Midnight.

Somehow, the boy manages to hobble and blindfold the horse, saddle it, and ride toward town. Along the way, a renegade Indian chief attacks, Midnight stomps him to death, then goes on to town where the doctor is found, whose operation saves the father's life. Somehow, the heated run has cured whatever ailed the horse, so the story ends happily.

Two weeks after I mailed the story, I received a letter from the editorial director of Popular Publications,

ROGERS TERRILL

"I like your story "King of the Redland Canyons" and am buying it for *New Western Magazine,*" he wrote. "You've developed good human characterizations, and I thought your horse color was excellent. Our check for thirty dollars will be along shortly. Send us more."

As I learned later, Henry and Harry Steeger, who owned the chain of detective, western, sports, and adventure magazines, expected to sell two hundred thousand copies of each title, making a net profit of three hundred dollars on each, a tidy sum overall but leaving little leeway in the operating budget for individual magazines. Rates paid to writers began at two-thirds of a cent per word. The chain Louis L'Amour was writing for at the time paid only one-half cent, so for a while at least, I was paid better than he was. In the western field, Popular Publications' lowest ranking mag paid the minimum, with the top rate of three cents a word in the best magazine, *Dime Western,* going to well-established names like Walt Coburn, Ed Earl Repp, and Eli Colter.

Trade talk had it that Ed Earl Repp, who appeared in many magazines, took stories written by young writers, paid them a penny a word, smoothed them out into his style, then pocketed two cents a word as they were published under his name. Of course, the only thing I was interested in at the time was that I had sold a story to a national magazine and was now a professional writer, well on the road to becoming rich and famous. But I still had many lessons to learn, and it was Rogers Terrill who became my teacher.

Setting aside my prejudice against shoot-em-ups, I began to write them, stretching them to the 12,500-word novelette length because more words meant more money. A couple of weeks after I mailed two of them, I received a letter from Terrill that, as the Victorian novelists used to say, gave me pause.

"We're accepting your stories, which are adequate for *Big Book Western*, though they're not very fresh or original. Our check for $280 will be in the mail shortly. But I think it's a shame that a young man who writes as well as you do should waste his time on these potboilers."

Immediately after the check arrived and was deposited in the bank, I wrote Terrill saying, "Thanks for the check and the kick in the rear. I hereby make you a solemn promise. I will write no more potboilers."

And I never did. From that day on, every story I sent him was the best I could possibly do with the material at hand. During the next couple of years, I gradually moved up into the better-paying magazines such as *Dime Western, Adventure,* and *Argosy*, with my rate increasing to two, three, and even five cents a word. Finally, the agent I had just acquired sent what she thought was a particularly good story to a slick-paper magazine, *Liberty*, which bought it for $350, seven cents a word. From that time on, most of my stories were submitted to *Liberty, Colliers*, or the *Saturday Evening Post*, with which Popular Publications could not compete. Though he had lost me as a regular contributor, no one was more pleased with my climb up the ladder than Rogers Terrill. He had finally kicked me upstairs.

Wanting to meet him and my new agent, Nancy Parker, as well as other editors I was contacting, I went to New York City in early October 1943, rented a small apartment in Greenwich Village, and lived there until May 1944. Though my apartment was a fifth floor walk-up, my servicemen buddies and I found the stairs no handicap, for we were young, single, and healthy—as were the girls living on every floor, whose doors were often open—and I had a spare bed for guests. During my stay there I got better acquainted with magazine editors such as Mike Tilden at *Dime Western*, Ken White at *Adventure*, Kay Bourne, fiction editor at *Liberty*, and two rising stars in the book field, Ken McCormick,

Doubleday, and Harwick Mosely, Houghton Mifflin, who later became my publishers and friends, and, of course, Rogers Terrill, the head man at Popular Publications.

Unconsciously, we had a rating system in our relationship, it being understood that lunch with Mike Tilden or Ken White was Dutch-treat, for their author entertainment budget was small; McCormick and Mosely were good for an end-of-the-day cocktail; Rogers Terrill would now and then take me to lunch at the glamorous Pen and Pencil on 42nd Street; while my lovely agent, Nancy Parker, whose husband, Captain Temple Fielding, was in the OSS and not home very much, would give me a call when in need of a single man to be her escort for dinner in the Village or a night on the town.

A rather short, chubby man with an endless supply of energy, Terrill somehow managed to keep thirty-three magazines profitable for Henry and Harry Steeger, while at the same time maintaining a personal interest in the careers of young writers like myself. No matter how far I strayed from the traditional western story plot line, he would consider and often buy the story if he liked it. On one occasion when I sent him a story about a happy-go-lucky Mexican, Juan, and his horse, Diablo, both of whom liked tequila and hated work, he bought it, saying, "I don't usually go for tall tales, but this one is so well done I've got to have it."

In this more enlightened day of political correctness, both he and I would be castigated, I'm sure, for relating the tequila-fueled adventures of this worthless pair, but the yarns ran as a popular series for half a dozen episodes in *10-Story Western Magazine*, moved up into *Liberty* for half a dozen more, eventually getting me involved in a proposed television series for which I received some option money and wrote a couple of treatments, though the series never made it to the tube.

On one occasion during a lunch at the Pen and Pencil, Terrill asked me what I was working on. "I started a story about a young Swedish immigrant who can't speak a word of English," I told him. "On the New York waterfront, he gets impressed into the United States Army, goes west, and is killed in a battle fighting for a country that has treated him badly."

"That was typical of our frontier army, wasn't it?"

"That's the point of the story. A lot of the soldiers couldn't speak English. The ending was so downbeat, I knew it wouldn't sell. So I abandoned it."

"Finish the story, Bill. I want to read it."

I did and he bought it, publishing it under the title "The Shining, Bloody Ground."

During my stay in New York, I often stopped by a neighborhood bar in Greenwich Village where I chatted with the middle-aged bartender about the progress of our war in Japan. One evening, he said, "World War II started long before Pearl Harbor, you know. In fact, I was in the first battle in 1935."

"Where was that?"

"On the Yangtze River in China. I was on the gunboat *Panoy* when it got shelled by the Japs."

While serving a hitch in the navy, he said, his gunboat came under fire from a Chinese fort ashore that had been taken over by the Japanese following their invasion of the mainland. Though I vaguely recalled reading about the incident and thought he had his facts mixed up a bit, I listened to his story without disputing it, forgetting it until years later when I was reminded of it in a rather curious way.

In the early 1950s, Rogers Terrill resigned as editorial director of Popular Publications and established his own literary agency. By then Nancy Parker had quit the business and moved to Majorca with her husband to start the *Fielding Guidebook* series. Though I now had Carl Brandt, Sr. as my agent, I had kept in touch with Terrill and sent him several clients. Now, I was reminded of my Greenwich Village bartender friend by a best-selling novel, and eight-part *Saturday Evening Post* serial, and a hit movie starring Steve McQueen titled *The Sand Pebbles*.

Taking a rough, crude manuscript written by a sailor aboard a fictional gunship called *The Sand Pebbles*, a New York literary agent had shaped the story into the success it became. The agent's name was Rogers Terrill.

Whether or not the ex-sailor was my bartender friend, I never learned, for shortly after the book came out Terrill died of a sudden heart attack. The publishing world lost a great editor, and I the good friend who had kicked me upstairs.

ERD BRANDT

The month I met Jeanne, my bride-to-be, I sold two stories to *Liberty* for a total of fifteen hundred dollars, my rate having gone up to fifteen cents a word. Born and raised in Tacoma, Washington, to which I had migrated after the war, Jeanne had never been east of Wyoming. Finding my tales of Greenwich Village and life in New York intriguing, she readily accepted my offer to take her there. Three thousand miles, three weeks, and two used cars later, we arrived in New York City in early October 1946, moving in with a writer friend and his wife who were leasing a small, rent-controlled apartment in Greenwich Village.

My agent, Nancy Parker, said the fiction editor of *Liberty*, Kay Bourne, wanted to see me and buy us lunch next Monday at an expensive restaurant uptown as a "welcome-to-New-York" greeting. But, as I relished the veal scaloppini, Miss Bourne told me the bad news. Engaged in bitter competition for circulation and advertising with the *Saturday Evening Post* and *Colliers*, *Liberty* was running a poor third. Drastic measures must be taken if the magazine were to survive. One of those measures was to quit buying stories from writers like me.

This meant I must go back to the pulps where I still had a few editor friends and be content with two hundred dollars or less for a story. To make our financial matters worse, Jeanne had quit a good-paying job in Tacoma where she worked in the office of the manager of the

Weyerhaeuser Steamship Company. She assumed that a writer earning big money like I was could support her in style. Housing was tight in rent-controlled New York, with apartments available only to renters who would slip a few thousand dollars in cash under the table to the current leaser or buy his wife a mink coat.

After answering ads in the Village paper without success for two weeks, we finally agreed to look at a remodeled New England farmhouse in the Berkshires near Pittsfield, Massachusetts, 150 miles north of New York City. The owners said they would rent it to a "responsible couple" for sixty dollars a month just to keep it heated and the new plaster from cracking during the cold winter months. The surrounding hills, we found, looked a lot like those we had left in Tacoma, three thousand miles away. But it was the best we could afford, so we signed a nine-month lease and moved in, saying New York City was only a half-day's travel away by car or commuter train and we could always run in if a friendly editor beckoned.

No editor did for the next couple of months as I went back to the lower-paying pulp markets where my chair at the table had been taken away by one of the dozen hungry writers always ready to replace the established regular who has been feeding there. By mid-December, we were hurting financially, but I had just finished a short story I thought might have a shot at the *Saturday Evening Post*, which had been showing an interest in my work. Taking place as trapping days are ending and travel beginning on the Oregon Trail, its hero is a shy young mountain man name Charley Smith who agrees to guide a wagon train to Oregon because he is smitten with a pretty young lady named Susan. This disgusts his Cayuse Indian partner, Bear Claw, who tells him he has a bad case of squaw fever, the only cure for which is getting a squaw. If Charley will forget his infatuation with Susan, Bear Claw says, he will introduce him to a number of nice young Indian girls who won't cost him too many horses if he'll let Bear Claw do the bargaining. But Charley disagrees, saying he wants a white wife.

As they travel out on the trail, the emigrants are joined by a detach-ment of cavalry commanded by an officious lieutenant who soon replaces Charley in Susan's affections. Thinking his army maps are bet-ter than Charley's knowledge of the country, he takes over as guide, eventually leading the train on a short-cut that proves to be a disaster, the wagons facing a one-thousand-foot drop-off in desert country with not enough rope available to lower them to the valley below. In despera-tion, the emigrants ask Charley for advice. He tells them, "You've got plenty of rope—you just don't recognize it when it's walking around."

He slaps an oxen on the back and tells the pilgrims how leather lari-ats are made. Because he has saved the wagon train, Charley gets the girl and they live happily ever after. As a courtesy to my bride of six months, I asked Jeanne to read the story and tell me what she thought of it. She did, then said, "It's a good story, Bill, except for the ending."

"What's wrong with the ending?"

"If Charley marries Susan, he'll have to start living like a white man. She'll henpeck him to death, making him fetch and carry for her father and mother and her lazy brothers and sisters. That's a poor way to reward Charley."

"How should I reward him?"

"Bear Claw says he knows a lot of nice Indian girls. Why not have him find one for Charley?"

"But that would be miscegenation. A slick magazine like the *Post* would never buy that kind of story. Besides, if I gave it that ending I'd have to open it up and add several scenes, which would make it too long for the *Post*. What you suggest just can't be done."

"Well, if you don't want my opinion," she said, "don't ask for it."

Just to show her how little she knew about the writing world, I opened up the story and added several scenes, the key one being where the wagon train gets to Cayuse country and a pretty young Indian girl carrying a new baby approaches Charley, smiles, and says, "Look what we got, Charley. Fat baby boy."

Susan and her parents were horrified, thinking the child to be his, so they ran him out of camp. Bear Claw is waiting, ready to help Charley pick out a nice Indian girl. The baby, of course, is Bear Claw's and the squaw his wife.

The new version ran ten thousand words, which would be another strike against it at the *Post*. Jeanne thought it a much better story, and, frankly, so did I. When I sent it to Nancy, her reaction was negative as she commented, "I'm not too sanguine about this one, though it's well written. I'll send it to the *Post* and let you know Erd Brandt's decision."

In those days, any story that reached the desk of fiction editor Erd Brandt, or his two associates, Stuart Rose and Robert Murphy, got a "Yes" or "No" within forty-eight hours. Our farmhouse was at the end of a country road that the snowplows sometimes did not reach for days. Our phone was also at the end of the party line, our ring being three longs and two shorts. When Nancy wanted to give us the good news of a sale, she would send it Western Union, the operator reading the message to us. Most of the time for the past two months, our ring had not sounded very often, though time and again we had waited with bated breath through three longs, one short—and then silence.

With Christmas near, our supply of cash was almost exhausted. We were low on groceries and completely out of wine and cigarettes. In West Stockbridge, the nearest village, cigarettes and wine could be purchased at the liquor store only with cash, but the friendly village grocer would let us charge food staples for a reasonable length of time. What should we do? After discussing the matter solemnly, we made the right decision, of course: We charged our groceries and spent our remaining cash on wine and cigarettes.

When we got home, the phone was ringing. Three longs, a short, a pause, then another short. The Western Union operator read me Nancy's telegram.: POST BOUGHT SQUAW FEVER FOR SEVEN HUNDRED AND FIFTY DOLLARS. ERD BRANDT WANTS TO MEET YOU. LETTER FOLLOWS. MERRY CHRISTMAS.

Indeed, it was.

At that time, the editorial offices of the *Post* were in Philadelphia, but once a week Erd Brandt or one of his associates came by train to New York and spent the day talking to writers. In early January, Erd would be making the trip, Nancy wrote, and would like to see me. So we drove into the city and checked into the Great Northern Hotel at 59th Street and Eighth Avenue, splurging three dollars a night for a room at the hotel where our landlords lived, making ready to meet the man who had given us such a happy holiday.

When I met Nancy at the midtown office building where the *Post* fiction editor conferred with writers, she told me, "You'll probably find Erd Brandt a hard man to talk to. He doesn't have much small talk, he mumbles a lot, and he jumps so fast from subject to subject that he's hard to follow. But I'll try to keep the conversation going."

Boston-raised and educated at Radcliffe, Nancy Parker was charm personified, having been a secretary to Fulton Oursler and a partner with Cornelius Vanderbilt, Jr., who had put up money to establish the agency, then turned it over to her to run when he went on to other things. We were slated for a thirty minute session, she said, but she would help me fill the time.

A tall, rawboned man with a craggy face, Brandt was in his mid-fifties, wearing a rumpled suit and a quizzical expression as if he had misplaced something recently and was trying to remember where he put it. After greeting Nancy, he shook my hand and said, "That was a mighty good story you sent us, Bill. Different and fresh. You're from Washington State, right?"

"Yes sir. From Tacoma."

"I've traveled all over that country. In fact, the first check I ever saw for one hundred dollars was made out to a man I met in Colfax, Washington. Do you know where Colfax is?"

"East of the mountains, in wheat country. I'll bet the check was made out to a wheat farmer."

"It sure was!" he said with a laugh. "His place covered several thousand acres."

We started talking about the Pacific Northwest, the Oregon Trail, mountain men, historical novels and nonfiction books we had read, jumping from subject to subject so fast that we soon lost Nancy, who just sat there and listened. Shrewd agent that she was, she did not interrupt, for, truth was, she could not have gotten a word in edgewise if she had tried. Somewhere along the way I had mentioned rewriting the ending to please my wife, to which Brandt replied, "Good thing you did. I wouldn't have bought the earlier version."

So far as the length was concerned, it was awkward, he said. "But we'll find a way to work it in." Miscegenation a problem? No way. "The *Post* will publish a story on any subject if it's handled properly."

Just before the session ended, he asked, "Bill, have you ever written a serial?"

"No."

"Would you like to write one for the *Saturday Evening Post*?"

"I certainly would."

"When you get back to Washington, see if you can come up with an idea for a serial set in the Pacific Northwest. I'd like something fresh, and I think you can write it. Let me know when you come up with an idea and I'll work with you on it."

That was the beginning of my fourteen-year relationship with the *Saturday Evening Post* and Erd Brandt, the finest editor I ever knew.

When we got home, I spent most of the next year researching the history of the Pacific Northwest, particularly as it related to the country east of the Cascades and the gold rush to it in the early 1860s, and writing an eighty thousand-word novel titled *Bend of the Snake*, which I hoped the *Post* would buy as an eight-part serial. But Erd turned it down, saying, "You've swung too big a loop, Bill. Good as the novel is, it's not right as a serial for the *Post*. Try us with something smaller."

After rejecting a major effort with a letter to the agent explaining his reasons, Erd often would write a personal note, scribbled in pencil, to the author, softening the blow by telling the writer exactly why he was turning down the story and encouraging him to submit something more suitable to the needs of the magazine. In a few months, I did, writing a taut, simple story about two young men trying to make a new life for themselves in a new western town, one by hard work, the other by violence, and how they fight on the same side like the brothers they turn out to be in the crisis shoot-out. Taking a month to write, it ran twenty-five thousand words. The *Post* bought it for five thousand dollars, publishing it as a three-part serial under the title *The Man From Texas*. Later, the longer manuscript was accepted by Houghton Mifflin as a novel, sold to the movies, and was filmed as a starring vehicle for James Stewart under the title *Bend of the River*.

When a story came close but was not quite right, Erd would dictate a detailed letter telling what was wrong and how to fix it, concluding, "If you do this, I'll look at it again." I always did and always made a sale.

During the years I was a regular contributor to the magazine, one or another of its fiction editors came out to the West Coast each spring, spending several days in Seattle, Portland, San Francisco, and Los Angeles, inviting each of their authors to meet them in the most convenient city for an hour-long session, a lunch, a dinner, or sometimes as a group during the evening, while the *Post* picked up the tab to send their wives and children to the movies. Before parting with the author, the editor would say, "Now Bill, if you have any problems or questions, phone me collect in Philadelphia."

Erd did not like to fly so he made the long trip by train, now and then bringing his wife along for company. In one unforgettable experience, I had just finished a story and was about to send it to the *Post*.

"Let me see it," said Erd. "I'll read it now."

And he did, and while his wife sat knitting, mine made small talk with her. I tried to act casual about the whole affair, though his yes or no meant twenty-five hundred dollars to us. Finishing the story, Erd scribbled a penciled note, gave it to me, then said, "I'm sending your story back to Stu and Bob for their opinion. This is what I'm telling them."

Stu & Bob: This is a good story of its kind. I think we should consider it.

By then, I learned that his approval alone was enough for a sale, but he would go along with their decision if the story got two votes from his associates. This one did not, so I made no sale. But during those hallowed fourteen years I was a regular with the magazine, with my rate climbing to fifty cents a word. I sold them enough stories to buy several new cars, one of which we named Benjamin in honor of the founder of the *Post*, Benjamin Franklin. When I told Erd that as he walked us to the parking lot in Portland one warm April day after buying us lunch, he laughed and said, "Well, if the *Post* can't supply you with milk, maybe we can buy you a little cream now and then."

Which it certainly did.

CARL BRANDT, SR.

When Nancy Parker retired from the agency business to work with her husband, I wrote several editor friends asking them for the names of three agents they liked to work with. Number One on every list was Carl Brandt, Erd's older brother, the literary representative who overcame the antipathy of George Horace Lorimer against agents. Lorimer was the legendary editor who made the *Saturday Evening Post* the great magazine it became. Obtaining letters of introduction from writer friends Tommy Thompson, Robert Ormond Case, and John Hawkins, all of whom were Brandt clients, I wrote and asked if he would take me on.

"I like your work and Erd speaks well of you," he replied. "Why don't you send me three of your stories that haven't sold so I can get an idea of how you write."

I did so, also sending him a few stories that had sold because I could not bear the thought of his reading only my clinkers. After a week or two, he replied, "Why don't we try it for a while and see how it works out."

As of this writing I am still with the agency, working now with Carl Brandt, Jr., who tells me I am his oldest client, though he implies our relationship is still "on trial."

Though it took me several years to realize it, Carl Brandt, Sr. was as good an editor as his younger brother, Erd, who would not buy a story from his own brother unless he liked it.

Here is one example of Carl Brandt's skills. In 1954 Jeanne and I wintered in Tucson, where I poked at story ideas each morning, then played golf or watched the Cleveland Indians' spring training games in the afternoon. Browsing through a reprint of the mountain man classic, *Ruxton of the Rockies*, I stumbled on a story idea begging to be written.

In the 1830s, Ruxton noted, a band of mountain men led by Joe Walker had crossed the Sierras and wintered in California, taking over a mission run by a friendly priest, whiling away their time by drinking wine, chasing señoritas, baiting bears, fighting bulls, and having a high old time, capping off the winter by stealing a few hundred horses to trade to the Indians when they re-crossed the mountains. Adding a few fictional characters to flesh out the plot, such as a Spanish *hidalgo* searching for an island of solid gold and great deeds to do, a romance between a pretty native girl and a young mountain man, and a murder attempt by a jealous rival, I concocted a story I called *Conquest* that demanded a length I had come to like, the "novella" of twenty-five thousand words, enough room to develop characters and tell a well-rounded story while still maintaining the tautness of the novelette length.

Ten days before we were scheduled to leave Tucson and drive back to Walla Walla, I mailed it to Carl, saying if I didn't hear from him before we left, I assumed I would soon after we got home. We had no phone in our rented house, but the day before we planned to leave, I got a telegram from Carl saying:

POST INTERESTED IN "CONQUEST" BUT SAYS IT NEEDS CUTTING. PHONE ME

Driving a mile or so to the home of a new friend, Leslie Ernenwein, who had recently persuaded me to join an organization called Western Writers of America, I used his phone to call Carl.

"The *Post* likes the story but can't use it in its present length. It's not the sort of thing that can be broken into a serial and the novelettes they publish can't go over 12,500 words. Do you mind if I work on it this weekend and see if I can't cut it to that length?"

"But, Carl," I said, "that's a rewrite, not a cutting job. Send it back to me and I'll work on it after we get home."

"Oh, no need to do that. I've had a little experience with cutting jobs. Let me take a whack at it."

"Go ahead if you like. We were planning to leave for home tomorrow, but we'll stay here for a while and I'll help you all I can."

"No need to change your plans, Bill. I'll get on with it and let you know how it works out."

An hour or so before we left Tucson the next morning, I got another telegram from Carl saying:

CAN YOU PUT FIRST NINE PAGES TELLING WHY MOUNTAIN MEN ARE LEAVING JACKSON HOLE TO GO TO CALIFORNIA INTO ONE PARAGRAPH FOR ME? WIRE SOONEST.

Recalling my experience with Foster Harris many years earlier when I had to reduce five-and-a-half pages of beautiful prose to a paragraph beginning, "Drawing his gun, he turned . . . ," it was not much of a chore for me to write and telegraph a new opening sentence, which declared, "After losing all their traps and possibles in a fracas with Indians, Joe Walker and his merry band of mountain men decided this might be a good year to spend the winter in sunny California . . ."

Stopping at Las Vegas and Reno to donate money to the crap tables and slot machines, then in Santa Rosa, California, to see Tommy and June Thompson, and in Bend, Oregon, to visit Dwight and Maryjane Newton, we took a week to drive home. Shortly after our arrival there, we received a letter from Carl Brandt, saying, "Cut *Conquest* to 12,500 words and sold it to the *Post* for $3,750. By the time I finished, the manuscript was so messy I had to have it retyped at a cost of $16.50. Hope you don't mind paying the extra charge."

I didn't.

When I told the story to Robert Ormond Case a year or so later, he laughed and said, "You were smarter than I was. When he offered to do the same kind of job for me on a *Colliers* story, I told him he could try, but I was so sure he couldn't do it I'd eat my straw hat if the mag would buy it. A few days later he wired me."

GET OUT THE CREAM AND SUGAR AND START EATING. SOLD THE STORY.

GORDON GIPSON

Though he never blue-penciled a single word I wrote for Caxton, Gordon Gipson, owner of that highly respected press deserves a place on my list of great editors, for he had the sterling virtue of knowing when *not* to edit a manuscript. Located in the small town of Caldwell, Idaho, twenty miles west of Boise, Caxton had published Western Americana for years. Though we knew each other's books,

Gordon and I did not meet until June 1969, when he came to a Western Writers of America convention in Medford, Oregon, to accept a Spur Award for the Vardis Fisher nonfiction book *Gold Rushes and Mining Camps of the Early West*, the author having passed away the previous year.

Over drinks, Gipson said, "I like your novels but we don't publish fiction. If you ever get an idea for a nonfiction book let me know."

By odd coincidence, the notion of writing a nonfiction book had come to me two years earlier when I wondered why *The Rivers of America* series had never done the Snake, the sixth largest river in the country. Though I was not a nonfiction writer, I put together a thirty-one page outline of how I could write such a book, sent it to Carl Brandt, Jr., and asked him to shop it around among eastern publishers.

None of them were interested. Checking with their sales reps, the editors learned that the total population of the one hundred nine thousand square-mile watershed was only seven hundred-fifty thousand people, less than several eastern cities. One editor facetiously asked Carl, "How many literate cowboys, Indians, and sheepherders have they got out there who would buy books?"

So, I put the outline aside and went back to writing fiction. Over a second scotch and soda, I told Gordon about my nonfiction book outline. "Sounds interesting," he said. "Send it to me."

I did, he went for it, and Caxton published a beautiful coffee-table-size book called *Snake River Country,* which has sold thirty thousand copies and is in its fifth printing thirty-four years later. Eventually, I would write nine books for Caxton, all of them still in print. Until his retirement a few years ago, Gordon Gipson had an editorial hand in all of them, though he never touched a word of text.

In 1980 I wrote *Chief Joseph Country: Land of the Nez Percé*, telling the Indian side of this tribe's unique relations with the white world. When finished, the manuscript ran a monstrous three hundred thousand words. Telling me no one at Caxton had the skill to do the copyediting, Gordon asked me if I would mind working with Joe and Ruth Wilson, a couple retired from the *San Francisco Chronicle* where he had been an editor and she a reporter. I said I would be glad to and did, conferring with them frequently by letter and phone as we went through the manuscript and clarified the text without touching its total wordage. Going over to Caldwell and talking to Gordon, I got the feeling that he was uncomfortable with the book's length, though he hadn't said so.

"It's too long, isn't it?" I said.

"Well, it is a long book."

"Do you want me to cut it?"

"Would you mind?"

"Not if the book needs it. Will you tell me where to cut it?"

"Oh, I wouldn't dream of doing that! It's your book."

"What if I cut ten percent?"

"That would be good."

"Fifteen percent?"

"That would be even better."

"Twenty percent?"

"Oh, that would be perfect! But I want you to do it."

So Jeanne and I went back to Walla Walla and I spent the next two weeks going through the manuscript making the cuts. Using a red pencil and noting the number of lines cut at the bottom of each page, I made the big cuts first—the topics that had little to do with the tribe's conflicts, matters that did not need to be discussed in such detail, page cuts that would really reduce the bulk of the book.

Going back through the manuscript again, I used a green pencil to make paragraph cuts, then a third time with a yellow pencil making line and word cuts. When finished, the manuscript looked pretty messy, but totaling up the cuts I found I had reduced the book's length by 19 percent. I took the now two hundred forty thousand words back to Caldwell and a pleased Gordon Gipson.

Setting Jeanne up at a card table in a motel near the city park from which she could take a break, she transferred my cuts to the manuscript about to go to the printer. I spent days at the Caxton plant dictating photo captions into a tape recorder to be typed by a secretary, an idea Gordon had suggested that saved us a lot of tedious work. Again, he did not blue pencil a word himself, but his skills as an editor saved everybody concerned a great deal of time and effort.

When the book came out, I did not miss a single edited word.

After I'd written Carl Brandt about the editing job, he replied, "An experienced editor once told me that when cutting a book a person should look with suspicion at the last topic in a chapter, the last paragraph on a page, and the last sentence in a paragraph, for a writer tends to repeat himself."

Checking the cuts I made, I realized that was essentially what I had done.

Of course, the way Carl Brandt, Sr. had cut *Conquest* many years earlier had required a different technique, for he had been dealing with a story that was tightly written to begin with. What he had done was to reduce the number of themes from my novella from half a dozen to two or three, with the main emphasis on the love story. This changed the structure without destroying the story. Later, when the full version was published in book form as part of a collection, I restored its length, which changed its dramatic values back to what they originally had been. Still later, when I adapted it as a stage play and a movie script, its values were changed again, though in each version it worked as a story.

Jeanne Gulick

Including my late wife, Jeanne, in this list of great editors I have known would have surprised her, I'm sure. But during the fifty-five years she was with me, she read everything I wrote and influenced its final form significantly, though like Gordon Gipson, she never blue-penciled a word. Earlier in this essay, I related her contribution to *Squaw Fever*, the first story I sold to the *Post*. As she continued to read and judge my stories, her skills as an editor became more psychological than verbal, for she never said much. A lifted eyebrow, a frown, a slight smile, a chuckle, a headshake, a nod—these signs of approval or disapproval were about all I ever got out of her. This exasperated me at first, but as I began to learn the code, I accepted it and watched her closely for clues. Now and again when I wrote a truly outrageous scene, we would argue about it a bit. I would walk off grumbling about her criticism, then the next day I would rewrite the scene with only a slightly different twist. She would say, "That's better, Bill," and pretend that the new way was my idea, not hers.

After we got married, she quit her job as a secretary and began to do my research after I learned that she would rather spend her time in a library than go fishing or play golf with me. Eventually, she turned pro, working fifteen years as Pacific Northwest Librarian at Whitman College while the best I could do was catch my limit of trout now and then and achieve a ten-stroke handicap as an amateur golfer.

On one memorable occasion, I did force her to use both her secretarial skills and editorial judgment while on the road. In 1957 I sold a western novel, *Showdown in the Sun*, to Tyrone Power's independent production company, Copa, headed by producer Ted Richmond, for the then respectable sum of $13,500. While the handsome forty-four-year-old star was filming *Solomon and Sheba* in Spain, Richmond hired a screenwriter named Edmund North to write the shooting script, with my movie also to be filmed in Spain on a location resembling that described in the book, Arizona and northwest Mexico.

My book was purchased, I later learned, because it had two strong male leads that would give Power something to play against. Having been an assistant producer at Universal-International when my movie *Bend of the River* was made, Ted Richmond hoped to duplicate its box-office success. But in 1958, halfway through the filming of *Solomon and Sheba*, Power suffered a fatal heart attack, all his assets got tied up in court because of a dispute among his ex-wives, and the filming of my book was postponed indefinitely.

Meanwhile, I sold *Hallelujah Trail* to the Mirisch Company, and in the summer of 1964, I went on location for a week with its director John Sturges and a cast headed by Burt Lancaster. By that time, the legal matters had been ironed out, so producer Richmond, noting the publicity *Trail* was getting, phoned Sturges and told him he had the rights to another Bill Gulick book that he would like Sturges to start directing.

As I later got the story from my Hollywood agent, H. N. Swanson, Sturges, with whom I had developed a good relationship, read my first book, then the screenplay, then told Richmond, "It's a great book but a lousy screenplay. Why don't you hire Gulick to fix it."

So just before Labor Day, I got a phone call from Swanson saying that Richmond would like me to read the screenplay, tell him what was wrong with it and how I would fix it, then come down to Hollywood and talk about making a deal.

Since we wanted to visit my folks in the Los Angeles area and watch the shooting of *Trail* interiors in Hollywood, which Sturges invited me to do, I told Swanson to send me the screenplay. I would read it and write a critique for Richmond, then we would drive down via the inland route, arriving in a week or so. Because of a foul-up in Special Delivery mail, the script did not reach Walla Walla until 6:00 P.M. on the evening before we planned to leave. Telling Jeanne we could read it while traveling, I put it aside until we hit the road the next morning.

While Jeanne drove the 140 miles from Walla Walla to Baker, Oregon, I read the screenplay, gave it to her without comment, then drove the same distance to Jordan Valley while she read it. Stopping for gas and lunch, we discussed its faults, on which we were in agreement.

"In my book," I told her, "I have two strong men who begin as friends, become rivals for the same girl, and turn into bitter enemies. During the climax fight to save the silver mine and their fortunes, they come together again and fight on the same side. When the battle is over, one of them gets the girl, while the other rides off into the sunset. But the screenplay destroys that relationship entirely."

"It certainly does," Jeanne said. "In it, the hero never does anything wrong, while the villain simply wants to kill him because of an old grudge that is never really explained. Everything the villain does is so stupid and dumb and the hero has no problem defeating him. How would you fix it?"

"By throwing away the screenplay and going back to the relationship I established in the book."

"Is that what you're going to tell Richmond?"

"I'll phrase it more diplomatically, but that will be the essence of my critique."

"When are you going to write it?"

If we kept to our schedule, it would be 8:00 P.M. before we reached our stop for the night—Winnemucca, Nevada. By then, I would be bushed physically and mentally, wanting only a couple drinks, dinner, and bed. I think well creatively while driving, and ahead lay one hundred miles of straight desert highway with little traffic. In the trunk of the car we had a portable typewriter, paper, and carbon. Jeanne was a skilled typist who in times past had taken many letters from me.

"If I dig out the portable and dictate a letter while I drive, do you suppose you could type it with the portable on your lap?"

"If you don't hit too many bumps, I'm sure I could."

So for the next half hour, I dictated as she typed, creating a two-page critique telling Richmond in some detail what was wrong with the screenplay and how I would fix it. After we checked into the motel in Winnemucca a little before dark, we fixed drinks and I read proof on the letter, finding that Jeanne had done a better job typing than I had done phrasing, for I had begun, "I'm dictating this while driving across the Nevada desert on a portable typewriter . . ."

But Richmond must have understood the message, for when I kept my 2:00 P.M. appointment in his office in the MGM Building in Culver City, California, a week later, the letter was lying on his desk next to a framed, autographed photo of Tyrone Power. After a bit of small talk during which he asked me how I got along with John Sturges and Burt Lancaster, to which I responded "fine," he got straight down to business saying, "Bill, I think I've put my finger on what's wrong with the screenplay."

"What's that?"

"In your book, you have two men who start out as friends, become enemies when they fall for the same girl, then come back together again as friends during the climax fight for the silver mine. But the screenwriter changed the relationship so that there's no real conflict between them. What we've got to do is go back to your book and rewrite the story as you told it."

"Ted, I do believe you've put your finger on the problem," I said. "I'll be glad to work with you on it."

"Good! I'll call Swanson and set up a deal."

It was a half-hour drive from Culver City to Swanson's office on Sunset Boulevard in Hollywood. When I walked in, he was just concluding his conversation with Richmond, saying, "Thirty-five sounds about right. I'll pass the offer on to Bill and see what he thinks. We'll be in touch."

Hanging up, Swanson smiled at me and said, "Ted says he'll pay you thirty-five thousand dollars for writing a new screenplay, which he hopes you can do in six weeks. If you run into trouble, he says, he'll bring in an experienced screenwriter to help you."

"Don't tell him I said so," I told Swanson, "but when he brings in a screenwriter to help me, his troubles will really begin."

Taking Swanson's advice, we stayed in Southern California for a couple of weeks waiting for the deal to jell, but it never did. Before he could obtain the three million from the bank the production would cost, the producer had to sign John Sturges to direct and Burt Lancaster to star. Neither of them would commit themselves at that time. Mine was not a big enough name to impress the bankers. So, as Swanson was fond of saying, the deal "went to sleep." But, I could always say I had been offered three times as much to fix a bad screenplay based on my book as I had been paid for the book in the first place.

So there you have my experiences with six of the great editors I have known. Because I am still writing and still have a couple of books in the works, the list may eventually be expanded. Since I don't want to spoil them, I won't name the ones I'm working with now. Maybe in another fifty years when I finally retire . . . ∪

Buried Treasures of the Ozarks

Paulette Jiles

Paulette Jiles is the author of the best-selling Civil War novel *Enemy Women,* as well as various poetry volumes and travel books. Born in the Missouri Ozarks, she now lives on and operates a small ranch near Utopia, Texas, with two horses, a donkey, and assorted dogs and cats. She is at present working on her next novel.

Paulette Jiles
(Photo by Frank Brooke)

Creative writing is a matter of going in search of buried treasure. It's in your head. You light your way with handheld candles or cressets or flashlights. Somebody has been here ahead of you, no telling how long ago. There are no devices or secret maps or help from the outside. You have no idea where you are in relation to either the interstate or the polestar. There are very old footprints and drippings of candle grease and they lead away into passages that grow increasingly narrow.

I had a dream during a time when I was working very hard on some poetry that later went into a collection that won the Canadian Governor-General's Award. I dreamed I was searching for buried treasure. I was in a cave with walls of dull, ordinary limestone, carrying a flashlight. I came to a large chamber and there it was, a cartoon-like pirate's chest with its mouth open and blazing with light from some undefined source. The treasure was fish; brilliantly colored tropical fish moving about in the air as if it were water, spilling out of the chest and then into it again. I was taken up by an unsurpassed feeling of delight.

My cousin Susan Jiles Lawson and I have been riding the Ozark trails for many years, all seasons of the year, both when the dogwood is blooming and when the sweet gums are orange and magenta and plum-colored in the fall.

We ride with various other people when we meet up with them. They always tend to be the same people; for instance, Everett Walker. We come upon him and the Baileys and the old fellow who rides a black Tennessee walking horse, and others.

Once we came upon a cave mouth two stories high on Hurricane Creek in the Irish Wilderness. We scrambled up the rockfall to look into its dark interior, a cave floor that was jumbled and rocky and threatened even more roof collapses. It was a place to hide ammunition, or leave messages, or ambush the unwary traveler taking the trail down Hurricane Creek.

There is buried treasure everywhere and you are going in search of it on the page. It often seems as if you were on a path toward a perilous crossing, an interior river without a bottom or a bridge, but if you keep on the path or turn down the darkest passageway, you will come upon the story, the real story, bright as a clown fish.

Out of those many journeys, I found the main character for my book *Enemy Women*, Adair Colley. I also found lost tombstones of the Civil War, collapsed mill dams, old stone houses standing in painful abandonment where once there had been people, and a roaring mill-wheel and games of chance. I found the unappeasable grief of those who had lost everything and buried their dead in unmarked graves. In every myth and every fairy tale of a journey there are always guardians of the treasure. The guardians are earthbound and shouldered in stone; they are the creatures that would turn you back, spiral your mind into disorientation, burden you with sadness, wash out the river crossings and leave you stranded on the far shore while on the other side is light and treasure and games of chance, the faint fiddle strains of "Soldier's Joy."

Buried treasure is not always tropical fish or a story or a single artifact that says to you *Aha!* as it comes into the beam of your flashlight. The most innocuous object contains within it the real story, the one you have been ignoring in your hope of locating either the interstate or the polestar.

Last year I was visiting friends on the east coast of Mexico in the state of Veracruz. A large extended family, they live in a small city high in the tropical mountains; they have coffee plantations and a fine house and servants and four good Arab horses. Young Julio, a true horseman and explorer, and who is presently finishing his university degree in veterinary medicine, offered to take me high into the mountains on horseback on the old muleteer, trails carved deep into the soil by the mules. I was ready go at five in the morning.

Julio and I and Raphael, the man in charge, rode past an immense waterfall called Bola de Oro. We went on higher and higher into the Sierra Madre Oriental. The trail at first was well traveled and broad, but it grew increasingly narrow through forests of sapodilla and *haya* trees. At one point, the little Egyptian Arab mare I was riding threw her head back and struck me in the cheekbone such a blow that I saw stars. I was knocked out for about fifteen seconds, but I stayed on. Julio and Raphael considered this a minor inconvenience, and as long as I was still upright in the saddle, we forged on.

We left the villages where the houses were made of cinderblock, where there were banana trees and jacaranda and orchids. We went higher into the villages where the houses were made of planks and painted bright blue, and on the porches birds sang in handmade cages. The Spanish they spoke to us was accented with the ancient Nahuatl. The people watched us go by and nodded and said nothing. The trail began to crater; tropical rains had poured down and turned it into a ravine with sides of yellow clay and still we kept on. High above us was the Cofre de Peyrote, a peak of fourteen thousand feet, skirted with snow.

Now we were into the pines and the horses were digging in, clawing upward in the yellow waxy clay with their front hooves. The mountain people had used this trail for mule-trains, bringing their produce down for so many centuries that it had become a chute of rainy clay, or several chutes, braided between islands of stone. I began to realize I was suffering from altitude sickness. At every pause we looked back down toward the coast, and in the far distance was Xalapa. We were making the same journey as the explorer Hernan Cortez in his struggle up from the coast, over the Sierra Madre, toward Mexico City.

Finally it was impossible to go on, even leading the horses, and we turned and started back at about eight thousand feet, before we reached the level of the mists where the tropical air meets the cold of the snow-bound peak of Peyrote. There wasn't enough air.

On the return journey I refused to fall off. The huge soup-plate horn of the Mexican saddle was helpful in this respect. My eye was turning bright blue and a sodden black. Altitude sickness makes you thirsty, very thirsty, as well as faint. I was proud of myself. I had not asked to go back or complained once and had got off and struggled with the mare on foot up the worst of the mudslides without asking for help. It was the greatest and happiest adventure I had ever been on. I would have suffered two black eyes for the privilege of riding that ancient trail with two young men who knew the way. But I was fading fast and the altitude made my thirst a torment.

We came back down at last to one of the high mountain villages of the blue planks among the pines, with singing birds captured in straw cages. Julio got off and asked at a window if they had any juice to sell. The woman said no. He then asked if she had any bottled water, and she replied no again. Finally, Raphael asked, "What do you have?"

"I have a Pepsi," she said. She dug down into a cooler of sparkling ice and brought up the most miraculous thing, a large plastic bottle of half-frozen Pepsi.

On every journey, my hero or heroine grows faint with thirst and hunger and feels he or she can go no further. My hero or heroine is wounded and his or her companions are at a loss, they seek help. Lo! A fat witch appears in a shabby house of blue plank, claws down into her chest of buried treasures, and presents the protagonist with a magic elixir. I drank down the entire bottle sitting on my horse. It was life-giving. *Volvía a la vida.*

A magic elixir of some sort is one of the standard offerings in the cave of buried treasure at the end of a perilous journey. In the search for buried treasure, symbolism comes to us in packages, without effort, without grasping for it. It is the natural and inevitable consequence of the story of a quest. Adair pauses at the bank of a dangerous river crossing. At the far side is her home, her people, the man who is in search of her. The major takes the ferry across the Mississippi and music floats to him from the other shore in a strange language, *Carolan Goalach*, an ancient Celtic lullaby. When Adair is ill with fever, deep in a cave-like room in a prison hospital, a dipper of muddy Mississippi River water is offered to her and she drinks it down gratefully.

The bottle of Pepsi will reappear in a story when it is needed. Symbolism is a poor word for these things; correspondence is better.

The buried treasures are the correspondence my hero or heroine finds when he or she goes in search of his or her heart's desire, but they will only appear for the active protagonist, to the one who is on a quest. The fashionably ironic hero or heroine, brittle with the trendy attitudes of hauteur and indifference, whose reply to the world is *not this, not this*, doesn't have any need for correspondence, or music in a foreign language, or games of chance, or flashlights or clown fish. But that is another matter.

Once your protagonist is on a quest, the most wonderful things happen. She goes the wrong way. She takes the easiest passage and ends up back where she started, without a fish or a song or a cold drink. She bogs down, troubled by inane people and conversations concerning minor surgical procedures or the comparative prices of various brands of kitchen appliances when she wants to say, *My heart is broken* or *I must find my father.*

Storytelling is entirely a mental activity, and thus the search for what lies inside the mind, the pirate's chest, spilling out its wonderful correspondences, is perhaps more difficult than other disciplines. A painter has color, or at least something physical. Those in the theater work with other people who repeat and interpret their words or noises. Language is transparent and occurs entirely in thought. There are many people who are quite talented with language who cannot sustain the hours of unadulterated thinking that goes into storytelling. They turn aside at the darkest and most dangerous passages, the ones that leave you vulnerable before and behind. But some pause and then go on, and even the hesitation itself is a story, of a mind in the grip of both fear and desire, which is being invented in the mind of the storyteller.

And at the end of the story we come out again. Out of the broad mouth of the cave on Hurricane Creek, out to where companions are waiting with the horses, and the bright sunlight is boiling up around them in heat waves, and they are saying:

"What was in there?"

Old river courses. Blind fish. The prayers of the Cherokee. Evil. A woman offering a bottle of sparkling liquid. A man with a club to black your eye. A cast-iron skillet full of dump cake. Five Spanish milled dollars. A song in an unknown language. Betrayal. The polestar. Treasure. Emptiness.

The keys to the kingdom. ♄

The Western and Me

Elmer Kelton

Elmer Kelton, author of more than forty novels and a dozen nonfiction books, lives in San Angelo, Texas. He has been awarded the Western Writers of America Spur Award seven times and the National Cowboy Hall of Fame Western Heritage Award four times. He has been honored by the Texas Institute of Letters, the Western History Association, the Texas Book Festival, and others.

Elmer Kelton
(Photo by Jim Bean)

Among Kelton's best known works are *The Time It Never Rained*, called one of the best books written in the past century, *The Good Old Boys*, which was made into a movie starring Tommy Lee Jones, *The Wolf and the Buffalo*, *The Man Who Rode Midnight*, and a six-book fictional series based on the Texas Rangers.

My love of the literature of the West began before I was able to read, thanks to my mother's reading stories to me. We lived in a line camp on a ranch nine miles out of Crane, Texas. Sometimes she brought home a copy of *Ranch Romances* from the big stack of pulp magazines always on sale at the drugstore. If I was lucky, it would contain one of S.

Omar Barker's stories about a ranch boy named Mody Hunter, a sort of Huck Finn on horseback.

I had no idea that someday I would be writing western stories myself, and that Omar Barker would become a mentor and personal friend. I just knew that I enjoyed the heck out of Mody Hunter's adventures. In my imagination, I could put myself in them.

This, I think, is the key to fiction writing of any kind, the ability to bring readers vicariously into the story and make them feel like participants, sharing the adventures, sorrows, and joys of the characters as if they were their own.

Having been a schoolteacher, my mother taught me to read at age five, starting with labels on cans in the pantry. Before long I was negotiating the stories for myself and devouring the school library as well. I was always more of a reader than a cowboy, though I grew up around cattle, horses, and cowboys. Those were a powerful influence on what I chose to read, and later, to write.

The cowboys I knew tended to be good storytellers. As a boy I loved to listen to their yarns on the bunkhouse porch or around the fire at the chuckwagon. Most of their stories were true in spirit, though they might stray a little from the actual facts to make a good yarn better. Whatever storytelling ability I have is a legacy from these men, especially my father, and from the many writers whose works I absorbed through my skin. I cannot remember details of the stories I heard and read, but their echoes still influence my work.

At one point, my mother decided to try her hand at writing a story for *Ranch Romances*. She wrote it in pencil on a ruled tablet. I am sure she never submitted it for publication, and in later years she could not recall having done it at all. Seeing her try, however, might have been the spark that started me to thinking I might do it too.

I read a wide range of subject matter, almost anything that came to hand, but it was always stories of a western nature that held my interest most because they seemed to reflect the environment in which

I was growing up. The cowboys I knew did not lead the exciting lives of those in the books, perhaps, but I imagined they *could* have. When some people argued that the western stories were not realistic, I was not dissuaded. I saw *realistic* around me every day . . . doctoring for screwworms, digging postholes, fixing fences and windmills, riding horseback when I was sweating through my shirt or when my feet were freezing in the stirrups. The stories were better.

As *Hank the Cowdog* author John Erickson would say years later: Pulling calves from first-calf heifers was not the stuff of a John Wayne movie, but the movie was a lot more fun.

Because I loved so much to read stories, I began making up my own by the time I was eight or nine. I wrote them but did not show them around. It seemed sissy stuff to be composing make-believe yarns when boys my age were supposed to be trying to break a leg playing baseball or riding milk-pen calves. But I was never good at those activities. Being nearsighted, I could not see the ball until it hit me in the face. Pitching horses usually got rid of me with their first or second jump. I realized early that I was better at writing about such things than doing them.

I was fond of pulp magazines and the Big Little Books. A cousin introduced me to Zane Grey's writings when I was around twelve. I read all the works of J. Frank Dobie, the great Texas folklorist, and I consumed over and over Will James's fine cowboy and horse novels such as *Smoky* and *Scorpion*. A tremendously talented artist, James illustrated his own books. He could draw horses with pen and ink better than anyone, even Charlie Russell. For years I harbored dreams of becoming an artist, too, and illustrating my own books. The art eventually fell by the wayside, but the writing stuck.

I had a great literary legacy to draw from. In a sense, the classic western story is descended from Sir Walter Scott and his heroic tales about the age of chivalry. Zane Grey conceded his debt to Scott in the title of one of his books, *Knights of the Range*.

I have recently been introduced to the Icelandic sagas of a thousand years ago and find they have more than a little in common with the traditional western, that which deals with the mythical West. The Viking heroes of the Icelandic stories often were more deeply flawed, however, than most editors allowed western fictional heroes to be.

James Fenimore Cooper wrote fanciful adventures about Indian troubles in early colonial times, as in *The Last of the Mohicans*. Though the locales were eastern, they were about a time when the frontier was not far west of Plymouth Rock. His work has not weathered well over the years, but it was highly influential in its day. Cooper spawned many imitators who unfortunately had more ambition than talent.

Bret Harte's sentimental mining camp stories, such as "The Luck of Roaring Camp" and "Tennessee's Partner," rose well above the average of their time.

The western as we know it is still trying to outlive the wildly fanciful "penny dreadfuls" of the mid 1800s to the early 1900s, written by Ned Buntline and his contemporaries. Their heroes, often shamelessly exaggerated characters out of real life such as Buffalo Bill and Jesse James, engaged in all manner of grand heroics. They killed off vicious Indians and treacherous Mexicans by the score, and single-handedly rescued innocent white maidens from villains of every stripe. Unfortunately these pulp epics, usually hastily and poorly written, put a stigma on the western story that it has never completely escaped.

One bright spot in that period, besides Harte, was Charles A. Siringo's *A Texas Cowboy* (1885), regarded as nonfiction though one suspects that old Charlie might have improved on the facts here and there. It was written before the mythical cowboy's heroic image had been set in concrete. Charlie comes across as a very human figure, not always heroic and certainly not always provident.

Owen Wister gave the western an aura of respectability with his groundbreaking *The Virginian* in 1902. It set the pattern for the traditional strong, silent Gary Cooper-type hero who has been a staple of the traditional western ever since. It was about a cowboy who seemed never to be working cattle, but its theme was about a man's pride and sense of honor that he must uphold whatever the personal cost.

A year after *The Virginian*, Andy Adams published a plotless novel, *The Log of a Cowboy*, based on his own experiences driving cattle up the trail from Texas to Kansas. It has been the basis for just about every trail-drive novel written since. I have borrowed from it myself.

Then along came Zane Grey, B. M. Bower, H. H. Knibbs, William McLeod Raine, Charles Alden Selzer, and others who arrived early enough to see the Old West in its waning days. Eugene Manlove Rhodes was among the most literary of this period, setting his stories in New Mexico in a land he knew well and among people who were his friends. And not to be forgotten is a friend of mine from the pulp magazines, Walt Coburn, an Arizona cowboy who found punching a typewriter paid better than punching cattle.

As a boy I read all of these writers and was influenced by each to some degree. They convinced me that I should write about the West as I saw it, to portray the kind of people I knew and the environment that produced them.

A strong interest in history has led me to read literally hundreds of first-person reminiscences written by people who lived during the frontier era. An outstanding example in early Texas history is Noah Smithwick's *The Evolution of a State*. He was in Mexican Texas before the fall of the Alamo and wrote his memoirs in his old age.

My favorite cowboy autobiographies are *We Pointed Them North* by Teddy Blue Abbott and *Dakota Cowboy* by Ike Blasingame. Teddy Blue told it with the hide and hair still on, and it was an unusually frank book for its time. Blasingame saw the world around him with a clear eye and an analytical mind.

Reminiscences are not totally a male province. Sally Reynolds Matthews's *Interwoven* is a classic told from a ranch woman's viewpoint, covering the Civil War era and the Comanche-Kiowa incursions, which for a time pushed the Texas frontier back fifty to seventy-five miles. Agnes Morley Cleveland's *No Life for a Lady* is a standout book about a ranch woman's life in early New Mexico.

The western movies were another strong influence on me, though I came to love them for their own sake as popular American entertainment and accepted the fact that most presented an unrealistic image of the West. They simplistically stressed the action and romance but conveniently overlooked most of the unpleasantly gritty aspects of frontier life. In current terminology, they presented an alternative reality of their own. In the main, they distorted history to suit the needs of the stars, the story, and public demand. Even John Ford, the greatest western director of them all, never let history get in his way. I regard his *My Darling Clementine* as one of the two or three finest western films ever made. Its depiction of Wyatt Earp and the O.K. Corral, however, is about as far from historic fact as Oz is from Kansas.

I had my B western heroes: Buck Jones and Ken Maynard in the early years, Gene Autry, Hopalong Cassidy, and Roy Rogers later on. Purists have sometimes condemned the musical western as a travesty, but I always regarded it as simply a different aspect of that alternative reality that was the western film in general. It often succeeded better within its own standards and limitations than did grand epics of higher aspirations. If Gene Kelly could sing and dance in the rain to the accompaniment of a full (and presumably dry) orchestra, why couldn't Gene Autry sing and play his guitar on horseback? It was all fantasy anyway.

My early writing was mostly surreptitious. However, by the time I reached high school I knew I wanted to do it professionally. I took a journalism course and worked on the school newspaper for two years under the tutelage of an ex-cowboy turned professor, Paul Patterson, who encouraged me to study journalism at the University of Texas. That turned out to be some of the best advice I ever received.

My father, by then, had given up hope of ever making a good cowboy of me, though he had strong reservations about my choice of a career. He feared I would starve to death as a writer. At least a cowboy got his meals and a paycheck, small though they might be.

Graduating from high school at sixteen, I was able to get in some time at the university before going into the service in World War II. I eventually found myself in an infantry rifle company in Germany. Fortunately it was late in the European war and the worst of it was already over. In the occupation army at the end of the hostilities, I had enough time on my hands to take correspondence courses and to write a few stories. None ever found a publisher, but each gave me practice that I needed.

Returning to the university, I became serious about fiction writing with a view toward publication. In my spare time I sat at a portable typewriter, beating out short stories and mailing them to the various western pulp magazines. Many seemed to get home from the post office before I did. But again, each helped me learn to write a little better.

During this time I took lessons from many writers without their knowledge. After studying several books about the craft of writing fiction, I bought a large stack of magazines and went through the stories, analyzing them, dissecting them like a frog in a biology lab, even copying segments on a typewriter to get a feeling for the writer's use of words to build an image or create an emotion. In particular during this period I studied Ernest Haycox and Luke Short, Haycox for his fine literary touch within the traditional western formula, Short for his excellent characterization and narrative technique.

Like most writers, I collected a basketful of rejection slips. Fortunately, I began receiving brief letters from one editor telling me the shortcomings of each story and suggesting either corrections or abandonment, as the case may have been. This was Fanny Ellsworth, and the magazine was the same *Ranch Romances* from which my mother had read me years before.

Finally, in my final semester, she bought a story from me. I thought I had it made. I had no idea it would be a full year before she or anyone else bought another. Meanwhile I had lucked into a job as an agricultural reporter on the daily *San Angelo Standard-Times*, which fitted my rural background like a kid glove. The job paid the bills and fed my growing family so I did not have to depend on my fiction for a livelihood. I wrote for magazines at night and on weekends. After two or three more years I was finally selling most of the short stories and novelettes I had time to write.

About the time I began to feel comfortable, the pulp magazines started dying. That was partly because of changing consumer tastes but largely because television was replacing magazine fiction as an entertainment medium. I had acquired a New York agent, the late August Lenniger. He advised me to switch to paperback original novels, or I would soon be without an outlet for my work. He said western novels were enjoying a boom and all the publishers were looking for them. "Get yours written, and I'll get you some money," he said.

What happened to me was similar to what was happening to my friends in the livestock business. They would arrive at the auction with a load of cattle or sheep, only to be told, "You should have been here last week. The market has broken."

My novel came too late. The western market had become glutted. My masterpiece was rejected by everybody Gus sent it to for about a year. But somehow I have always been lucky in escaping from total wrecks of that sort. Ian and Betty Ballantine were establishing their own publishing company and looking for some new writers they might be able to build up. They bought my first book, *Hot Iron*. Over the next twelve or fourteen years they bought a dozen or so more.

What success I had in those early years I owed to two lady editors: Fanny Ellsworth and Betty Ballantine.

As happens in most industries, publishing got caught up in a wave of mergers and acquisitions. The Ballantines eventually sold their company to a large conglomerate. It bought a couple of books from me, but the personal rapport I had with the Ballantines was missing. Once again, I was lucky. I had become acquainted with Harold Kuebler, then the western editor for Doubleday. Harold asked me to write something for Doubleday's Double D Western series.

For several years I had harbored an idea of writing a novel about the cowboy strike at Tascosa, Texas, in 1883. I wrote it and submitted it as a conventional western of about sixty thousand words. Harold said something I had never heard before and don't believe I've heard since. He said, "Can you take it back and make it longer?"

He said if I expanded it successfully, Doubleday would feature it as a trade novel rather than as a conventional western. So I rewrote it, put more development into the principal characters, and altered the ending. It came out in hardcover as *The Day the Cowboys Quit*. It received some favorable critical attention and Harold asked what I would do for him next.

During seven years of the 1950s, Texas suffered through the worst drought anyone then living could remember. As an agricultural journalist, I wrote about dry weather almost every day for seven years. Eventually it struck me that this could be the basis of a novel if the drought ever broke, so I could know how the story would come out. It broke in 1957, one of the wettest years I ever saw. I wrote what I thought was the best thing I had ever done and entitled it *This Dry and Dusty Land*. The title alone was enough to kill it. It was roundly rejected everywhere it went. I rewrote it and tried again, with the same negative results. So I put it away and continued writing more conventional novels for Ballantine Books.

It was some ten years later when Harold asked me what I was going to write for him next. I then completely rewrote my drought novel from page one to the end, adding new sequences, expanding the characterizations, and giving more attention to racial problems that had prevailed in 1950s Texas. The result was *The Time It Never Rained*. The book received modest critical attention and acceptable sales at the time, but nothing spectacular.

Not until some years later when Texas Christian University Press republished it in an academic edition did it suddenly catch the attention of academia. It acquired considerably more stature in its second incarnation than in its first. For that I owe a third lady editor, Judy Alter. It has become my signature book. I have been trying for some thirty years to top it.

Wherever I go, I'm asked to talk about the writing process. Many people seem to think I should have worked it down to a science after more than fifty years. The truth is that I consider myself a perennial student, I keep learning new things or being reminded of old truths I once knew but had neglected or forgotten.

True, there are certain basic rules in fiction writing, though they are not inviolate. Often a writer breaks these rules for a good reason and with a good outcome. In the main, though, they are legitimate.

For me, the highest priority goes to characterization. I want the characters to seem real and for the readers to become emotionally involved with them, to care what happens to them. They may like a character, or they may dislike him. The main thing is that they care one way or the other, and that they become involved enough to stay with the story until they find out what happens to him.

There are many ways to develop and present individual characters, and most writers use several. Physical description is important, though it need not be carried to an extreme. Most readers quickly forget the fine details such as eye and hair color, which after all seldom have anything to do with what kind of person the character is—with the possible exception of redheads. Readers are more likely to remember those physical attributes that indicate character or that may have a bearing on what happens in the story. For instance, if a person is seeking retribution for an injury, the lasting results of that injury—say, a limp or a scar—are important. If a character's health is important to the story, the physical evidence of his or her condition is a vital piece of the description. The character's size and agility may be the key to his or her ability to meet a physical challenge.

Dialogue is another way to bring a character to living, breathing life. The way he or she speaks, the grammar or lack of it, the colloquialisms peculiar to a region or an occupation, can tell more about the person than a half-page of pure description. The teacher and the banker will express themselves differently than the cowboy or the truck driver or the high school kid who mows the lawn. Speech patterns are effective in enhancing the reader's vision of the character.

Seldom do I go through a question-and-answer session without someone asking me where I get my ideas. It is almost impossible to give an acceptable answer, because the ideas come from everywhere and nowhere. I have long been a student of history, especially of the West and in particular of Texas. Many of my story ideas come out of history. In particular I look for periods of change, when an old order is being challenged by the new. This sets up a natural field for conflict between advocates of the two opposing positions, those resisting change and those embracing it. Conflict of some kind is necessary if a story is to have any suspense. The reader has to invest emotion in the outcome, or the story goes flat.

Though usually the conflict is between people, it does not always have to be physical. It may be the natural differences that arise within a marriage, or between the generations within a family. It may be an inner conflict involving the character being torn between two choices, each of which carries a cost.

Another variation is man against nature. A sterling example is Jack London's *To Light a Fire*, in which a man's life depends upon his being able to start a fire with his last remaining match to avoid freezing. Another is Ernest Hemingway's *The Old Man and the Sea*. I have read stories about great armies in furious battle that did not move me half as much as my concern over whether Hemingway's old fisherman will be able to make it to port with the catch of his life.

I am in awe of writers who can do that.

Some stories cannot be accounted for. They just come out of the blue.

One piece of advice I always give to the young, aspiring writers is: Don't quit your day job.

I remained an agricultural journalist for forty-two years while also writing fiction. People have occasionally asked me if I regret it, for I could have written more books had I not been involved in newspaper work. But I saw the two parallel careers as complementing one another. The job gave me financial security so that each book was not a life-or-death matter. I was freer to write the kind of stories I wanted rather than tailor them to market demands with which I sometimes disagreed. It allowed me to experiment.

Moreover, my job kept me in constant contact with the kind of folks who populated my books. Often I could weave a book or at least a segment out of stories I heard during my many interviews with farmers and ranchers, especially in the case of *The Time It Never Rained* and *The Good Old Boys*. A writer should keep his or her antennae up all the time for material that can be turned into workable fiction. I usually take whatever liberties I need to fit my characters or the situation. Seldom do the people who inspire the stories recognize themselves. In one notable case, I borrowed the unfortunate experience of a man I knew quite well, a rancher who lost almost everything during the 1950s drought. I was a bit uneasy about his reaction should he happen to read the book and realize he was the principal model for the character Page Mauldin. Sure enough, I ran into him one day, and he said, "I just finished your book." I kept my eye on the door.

He said proudly, "You know, that Charlie Flagg was just like me." He never made the connection with the other character, and of course I never told him.

I am often asked about my writing routine: Do I write every day? Do I set a quota of so many hours or so many pages? If I am talking to young want-to-bes, I sometimes fudge and make myself sound more disciplined than I really am. It is important for beginning writers to develop a strong work habit because it is easy to put off doing today what can wait until tomorrow. I have heard so many people say they intend to write a book when they get the time. My experience is that they never *get* the time; you have to *make* the time. The longer a person waits, the less likely it is that he or she will ever actually do it. So I tell writing students to go home and start their book *tonight.* You'll find too many excuses if you put it off.

During my newspaper days I had to ration my writing time because of the demands of my job. Since my retirement from deadlines I have lost some of that discipline. I rationalize that I am old and tired, but that is probably something of a cop-out. I do try to write at least something every day when I am at home, though I am called upon to travel quite a bit making talks, doing book signings, and the like. I do not set quotas for myself. I do have a self-imposed deadline for finishing a book, well ahead of the contract date.

Another frequent question deals with planning and outlines. Certain writers I know outline a book in some detail on paper before they start. A few outline each individual chapter in even more detail. This works for them, and that is fine. It does not work for me. To me it is like working in a straitjacket. It discourages spontaneity. When I begin a new book I usually have a good idea where I intend the story to go and a concept of the ending. However, all this is subject to change as I go along. Characters have a tendency to grow and take on a life of their own as you work on them. Often what you originally intended for them no longer fits when you reach that point. If you start out on a trip but have no destination, you tend to wander aimlessly. But, if you start with a destination in mind and later change it along the way, you can still have a satisfactory trip.

Each writer has to find what works best for him or her.

A few times a character has taken a story away from me and run with it. A story has simply rolled out as if it had a life and a will of its own. People who have never tried to write fiction rarely understand that.

One of the best pieces of writing advice I ever received was from S. Omar Barker. He said if you write long enough you will develop a subconscious that does much of the work for you. Even when you are doing other things and supposedly not even thinking of the story, somewhere deep in your subconscious that story is slowly working, developing. Many times I have come to a dead end in writing a story and have not known where to go next. Later I may be driving down the road or reading a paper or eating lunch when suddenly the solution pops into my mind, seemingly out of nowhere. The subconscious has been working for me. I have learned to trust it, most of the time, so long as the solution it offers is plausible and fits the characters.

I have never liked to write about superheroes. I can enjoy them in other people's work, though I have to suspend disbelief and go along with the premise. I just can't take them seriously enough to write them into my own stories. I prefer to write about people I can understand, people like me and those I know, people who can sometimes be vulnerable so that the reader can be concerned about what may happen to them. I have sometimes said my characters are not seven feet tall and invincible; they are five feet eight and nervous. I know those characters. I have been in their shoes, or boots.

Most of the writers I know have been voracious readers from childhood. Anyone who does not love to read will probably not like to write.

If there are any shortcuts to learning, I have not found them. A prerequisite is to read, widely and copiously. One learns by studying other writers and their work, perhaps even modeling after them to some degree at first. In time each person will develop his or her own writing style, their own voice. There is no point in being a carbon copy of someone else. After all, a reader can buy the original for the same price as the copy.

Now and then someone will hit a home run with a first book, but this is rare. Most writers labor in the vineyards for a long time before they achieve any notable success. When young writers ask me the secret, I have to tell them there isn't one. At least I never found it. One learns to write by reading, and reading, and reading some more, and in writing, and writing, and writing some more, until it becomes second nature to put words on paper and give meaning to those words.

A beginning driver reads the manuals and learns the laws of the road, but eventually he must put his hands on the steering wheel. Libraries offer many worthwhile books on how to write. These can help a beginning writer avoid many of the pitfalls. But in the end he must sit down at the keyboard and go to work. That is when the real learning starts.

It should never stop. ∪

Writing the West

History, Geography, and Culture

Robert Utley

Since his retirement from the National Park Service and other federal agencies, Robert Utley has devoted himself full-time to historical research and writing. Ten of his books have been selections of the History Book Club, eight of the Book of the Month Club.

In 1988 Utley was awarded the Western History Association prize for distinguished published writings and in 1994 the same association's Caughey Prize for *The Lance and the Shield* as the best western book of 1993. In 1988, 1989, and 2003 he

Robert Utley
(Photo by Robert Utley)

received the Wrangler Award from the National Cowboy and Western Heritage Museum for his writings. In 1994 he won a Spur Award from the Western Writers of America and the Owen Wister Award for distinguished lifetime achievement. In 1997 the Society for Military History honored him with the Samuel Eliot Morison Prize.

Born in Arkansas in 1929, Utley was raised in Indiana, educated at Purdue University and Indiana University, and holds Honorary Doctor of Letters degrees from Purdue, the University of New Mexico, and Indiana University. He is married to Melody Webb and lives in Georgetown, Texas.

I am a historian of the American West. For me, geographically the West is the land lying west of the Mississippi River together with Alaska, the Canadian West, and the Mexican North. Others enlarge this definition to include the entire nation from Atlantic to Pacific, which allows the West to be examined in terms of process rather than region, for example, the westward movement of Euro-Americans across the continent. Many also add Hawaii. Chronologically, my region moves from the sixteenth through the twentieth centuries.

Both geographically and chronologically, my definitions do not represent consensus, just my personal interests. I am only marginally concerned with the West that lay east of the Mississippi, with Hawaii, and with aboriginal history before the advent of Europeans. I have worked almost altogether in the nineteenth century and specialized in Indians, soldiers, the Indian wars, Indian policy, mountain men, and outlaws and lawmen.

As a youth in Indiana, I got hooked on the West by those marvelous B westerns that hit the movie theaters in the late 1930s. The one most responsible for pointing me toward the West and its history and ultimately toward writing was *They Died With Their Boots On*, Errol Flynn's rendition of George Armstrong Custer "from West Point to points West."

That led to six summers during college with the National Park Service standing on Custer Hill telling visitors the story, 1947–52. That experience in turn led ultimately to a full-time career with the Park Service. After four years in the army, I came back to the Service as historian for the Southwest Region, based in Santa Fe, 1957–64. I then moved to Washington as chief historian, later as an assistant director, and finally as a deputy director of the President's Advisory Council on Historic Preservation, 1964–80.

Those summers at Custer Battlefield, however, afforded the setting for my first tentative step toward writing history—a brochure telling the story in print that sold at a souvenir shop outside the park. Self-financed and self-published at a thousand copies, it paid off its $350 investment but saddled me forever with an embarrassing exhibition of wretched prose. It sold for seventy-five cents and now occasionally turns up on a rare booklist for several hundred dollars. It no longer haunts me because it is long buried by what I think is better writing.

Amateurish as that enterprise was, it instilled in a nineteen-year-old not only unwarranted pride, but an ambition to see my name in print again. Throughout my Park Service career, however, writing had to be a sideline. After I took early retirement from the federal government in 1980, writing became a full-time preoccupation for me, as it remains to this day.

The West has always been my focus. Its past is full of a rich array of characters, but perhaps as important, it offers a rare setting for the kind of history I try to practice. This combines research in both indoor and outdoor archives to enable the reader to visualize a drama unfolding on a stage. It is what the National Park Service does through various interpreting media in presenting a historic place to the visitor. Despite urbanization and other development, the West still retains enough undamaged landscape to offer a stage for historic events.

Stand on Custer Hill, as I did for six summers, and scan a landscape only slightly changed since 1876. If you know the history, you can visualize the action that swept over that landscape. Or, to borrow a metaphor from Frederick Jackson Turner, stand at South Pass even today and watch the nineteenth-century version of the procession that threaded the Cumberland Gap a century earlier.

From the beginning, therefore, reinforced by my Park Service career, I have been a vocal proponent of combining indoor and outdoor research. Learn what happened from the indoor archives and libraries, then take it to the outdoor landscape, work out what happened where, and pen a narrative of people interacting with their geographical setting. A writer who can visualize the landscape, in large scenes or small, is better equipped to turn out vivid and accurate narrative than the practitioner who remains ensconced in archival caves. My embrace of both indoor and outdoor research testifies both to a vital technique and an abiding love of the West of yesterday.

The value and dynamics of this approach came to me early in my career with the Park Service, working the southwestern states from the Santa Fe office. We had several historic places proposed for addition to the National Park System, but an administration and a Congress unreceptive to new parks. Meantime, however, part of preparing a legislative package was the identification of historic sites to ensure that proposed boundaries included them.

My introduction to combining archival and landscape research focused on what eventually became Fort Bowie National Park in southeastern Arizona. Fort Bowie guarded Apache Pass and Apache Springs in the portal between the rugged Chiricahua and Dos Cabezas Mountains. It played a vital part in the Apache wars with Cochise and Geronimo.

The ending wall stubs and stone foundations of the fort's buildings seemed obvious enough, and the planners were content simply to draw boundary lines around them. But these remains survived from the second Fort Bowie. Where was the first? Where did the celebrated Bascom Affair of 1861 occur—the blunder of a green lieutenant George N. Bascom that drove Cochise into a decade of bloody warfare? Where was the Butterfield stage station that figured so prominently in that affair? Where were the sites of other events critical to understanding the Bascom Affair? Where, for that matter, did the Butterfield Trail make its way through the pass? Where were the warriors of Cochise and Mangas Coloradas posted in their battle with the advance guard of General James H. Carleton's "California Column" trying to reach the water of Apache Springs? Where was the Indian Agency building for Cochise after he made peace?

I immersed myself in archives at the then named Arizona Pioneers Historical Society in Tucson. Here were documents created by participants in all the events. With a sheaf of notes I headed for the Cactus Motel in Bowie and for days took my papers out to the fort. Estimates of distance from one place to another and descriptions of associated terrain narrowed the field. By comparing distance with terrain features, I could infer where things happened. The rock projections on the slope above the springs, for example, coincided with the testimony of soldiers who said they fired at Indians hidden behind rocks above the spring, and the lay of the land left only one area in which howitzers could be set up to bring the slope under fire.

A similar process led to finding other important sites, including the canyon location where Bascom and Cochise faced off, the stage station, and the presumptive Apache agency structure. With the use of historic military maps and modern aerial photographs, I identified the Butterfield Trail and walked its trace on the ground.

My superiors were not pleased to have to draw more inclusive boundaries, but they did. Finally the legislation passed. All seemed worth it on the day in 1972 when I joined with Congressman Morris Udall to dedicate the newly established Fort Bowie National Historic Site.

Fort Bowie remains memorable as my first successful experience with combining indoor and outdoor research. Another from my Santa Fe years is also revealing. It centered on a park proposed for the place where the transcontinental railroads joined at Promontory Summit, Utah. Hardly any more desolate place can be found. No tree, shrub, or other vegetation brightens the flat gap in the Promontory Mountains where the rails met. In 1960, the rails long gone for a war effort, a scruffy little concrete monument stood on the barren site. No one in my Park Service office believed such a dreary place belonged in the National Park System.

But the rails connected on a summit, which meant inclines on either side. No one from the Park Service had ever looked there. I did.

Snaking up the slopes, in dramatic illustration of the great railroad race, were parallel grades, cuts, fills, and trestle footings that testified to the battle between the Union Pacific and Central Pacific for government subsidies. The point of union had not been fixed when the two construction gangs reached the summit, so they continued to build side by side, enacting an exciting adventure in the process.

Fixing the elements of the story to the terrain was the historical challenge. In the Stanford University Library I found the best evidence—San Francisco newspapers containing the dispatches filed by their reporters on the scene. They described in detail what happened each day and where. Constructing the unfolding story along the parallel grades and hooking dramatic events to specific sites proved fun and not difficult at all. We drew the boundaries to include all the sites. Once again, with less than enthusiastic support from my office, the legislation made its way through Congress to produce a Golden Spike National Historic Site in time for the 1969 centennial.

These were youthful learning experiences. After my years as a Washington bureaucrat, I returned to the practice. For my history of the Lincoln County War and biography of Billy the Kid, I found my sources in southeastern New Mexico. It was not simply a case of identifying sites but getting a true feel for the topographical setting. I remember sitting in my car near old Fort Stanton writing descriptions of the terrain rolling down to Lincoln and up into the Capitan Mountains. For my biography of Sitting Bull, I visited all the important sites in the Dakotas and Montana and even made a sweep across the Canadian plains where Sitting Bull took refuge for four years after the Custer Battle. While living in Grand Teton National Park, I wrote my history of the mountain men. From that convenient base I untangled the incredibly complex geography of the northern Rockies. An understanding of those overlapping river systems and mountain chains is essential to an understanding of the story of the mountain men.

I call myself a narrative historian, one who narrates stories of people and events for the lay reader. A few university professors have achieved distinction as narrative historians, but most write what may be termed monographic history, that is, learned exegeses usually aimed at a particular interpretive thesis. These works are not intended for the lay reader but for other scholars in the academic world. Indeed, faculty promotion and ultimately tenure often depend on such writing, as commanded by the tired cliché, "Publish or Perish."

The two classes of historians have not always coexisted happily, if at all. Monographic historians are often accused of writing dense, unreadable prose solely for one another. Many respond by ridiculing narrative historians as superficially pandering to an undiscriminating popular market drawn by adventure, romance, and even legend.

My own view is this. Academic historians are doing what they want to do and what is necessary for advancement in their profession. Their writing is intended for their peers, not the outside world. They should be judged for their scholarship, not by their prose. And their scholarship, if sound, is vital to the narrative historian. However dull the writing, they have produced books and articles critical to my work. They have done much of my research for me, identified obscure sources, and provided insights and interpretations that may have eluded me.

All of which leads to the matter of documentation. Narrative history, as Francis Parkman demonstrated a century and a half ago, must rest on solid research and documentation. Otherwise it merits the contempt of academics. Books, magazines, and television are full of thinly researched outpourings that give the genre a bad name and highlight the necessity of solid documentation to support the readable prose.

Thus the documentation demands are the same for both monographic and narrative history. I believe in thorough research, indoor and outdoor. I believe in a rigorous test of plausibility: Is what the documents suggest likely to have happened given the people, time, and place? I believe in larding the narrative with my own interpretation of people and events. I believe in unceasing questioning and probing to close unexplained gaps the sources leave in an unfolding story. I believe in the footnote, or endnote, and the obligation not only to cite and evaluate sources, but in controversial issues to explain the reasoning that led from sources to text. In my biography of Billy the Kid, for example, I describe in three paragraphs his killing of Deputy James W. Bell during his famous escape from the hangman's noose, but such is the controversy that I use nine paragraphs in the endnotes to explain why I believe it happened as narrated. The endnote, moreover, should be used sparingly to add material that may be interesting but not enough so to include in the text.

I like to believe that I have a foot in two worlds, the popular and the academic. When I write, I aim for the popular reader. But I have discovered that there are enough professors who appreciate sound narrative history that every book I have written in the past forty years has won approving reviews in scholarly journals. The honorary degrees and a prominent role in the Western History Association testify to acceptance if not veneration by the academic world. As for the popular world, most of my books have been modest moneymakers, a couple comfortably more than modest. I have also gained prominence as a "talking head" in television documentaries that brings sudden recognition by strangers in almost any public place.

In an earlier passage I exempted monographic historians from writing readable prose. Since this is endemic, and few professors write interesting, clear, precise, jargon-free prose, it hardly seems fair to fault them for failing to teach their students how to write. But they don't, either because they can't or because they believe fledgling professors ought to be concentrating on thinking, interpreting, and teaching instead of on their writing style. Graduate programs are self-perpetuating engines for turning out generations of inferior writers.

I studied under Oscar Winther at Indiana University. He was one of the biggest names in western history at the time. He turned out highly respected works filled with sound content couched in dull prose, and he let me pack my master's thesis with execrable prose. Neither he nor any other professor ever uttered a word about style. For that failure I still hold them culpable.

For teaching me the rudiments of what I ought to have been taught at Indiana University, I credit three military officers: Air Force Major Norman E. Cawse-Morgan, Marine Major Ernest Guisti, and Army Captain Wilbur Hoare. In 1954, a newly minted second lieutenant, I managed to get myself transferred from the Infantry School at Fort Benning, Georgia, to the Historical Section, Joint Chiefs of Staff (JCS) in the Pentagon in Washington, D.C. It was four months after the French collapse at Dien Bien Phu in what we then called Indochina (today's Vietnam, Laos, and Cambodia). The United States was drifting toward taking the place of the French. The JCS chairman, Admiral Arthur Radford, wondered if historians might be good for something other than writing about World War II. He ordered a book-length study of the involvement of the JCS in Indochina. We worked night and day and weekends for four months and turned out a truly first-class history, based on highly classified documents. Within the Joint Staff it was a best-seller.

Those three officers, though lacking the terminal degree, were superb historians and stylists. They demanded and practiced rigorous analysis of sources, clarity, precision, and smooth narrative flow. They knew they had a novice to deal with but assigned me a chapter. I didn't know it, but from the beginning they conceived my assignment as a learning experience. With what anticipation they awaited the denouement I understood only later. When the time came for critique, they pounced in what I still recall as the most humiliating ordeal of my education. They demolished almost every paragraph and sentence, explaining why it was flawed, and how to remedy it. I recall in particular I had written that the United States aimed to short-circuit the French and funnel aid directly to the South Vietnamese. My critics then diagramed an electrical circuit to demonstrate that I had used the wrong metaphor.

At almost the same time I had the good fortune to become acquainted with an English professor at the University of Chicago, Norman Maclean. At the time he had a bright reputation as a teacher but had written little. Not until after his retirement did he win acclaim for *A River Runs Through It* and *Young Men and Fire*.

Norman Maclean was a Custer buff, and he proposed that we collaborate in writing a tribute to Captain Edward S. Luce, the tough old soldier who had recently retired as superintendent of the Custer Battlefield National Monument. The "collaboration" consisted of a collection of anecdotes by an apprentice historian crafted into a fine article by a seasoned writer. It appeared in the summer 1956 issue of *Montana the Magazine of Western History*.

Maclean tried for fifteen years to write a Custer book. He never succeeded, but during that period he and I developed a warm relationship, one in which he emerged as mentor and I as protégé. He thought I had high potential, and a file full of handwritten letters, some a dozen pages long, testify to the effort he invested in me. He led me through every sentence in the book that became *The Last Days of the Sioux Nation*. Thus, I add Norman Maclean to the three military mentors who laid the groundwork for my rise as a writer of comfortable distinction.

And, "defeated by defeat," as he put it in conceding his failure with Custer, Maclean turned to another defeat to win victory. *Young Men and Fire* dealt with smoke jumpers trapped on a blazing slope and wiped out. In this book, what he had wanted to express about Custer and his men doomed on another Montana slope finally brought liberation from the obsession that had gripped him for almost twenty years.

I turn now to an issue about which I feel very strongly. The technical term is "presentism"—the urge, even in scholarly practice, to judge earlier generations by today's standards and attitudes. For the past three decades this has been most evident in the history of Indian-white relations, but the "New Western History" that began to build momentum in the late 1890s has expanded it to include race, gender, and ethnicity—RGE—as well as the western environment itself.

The "Red Power" movement launched in 1968 by Vine Deloria with *Custer Died For Your Sins* gave impetus to the movement to redefine how we look on the behavior of westward-moving whites in the nineteenth century. Dee Brown wrote the bible in *Bury My Heart at Wounded Knee*. It was bad history but a powerful polemic that did more than any other single influence to change American thought. Indian activists—chiefly the American Indian Movement—agitated the issue through the 1970s and 1980s, both for restoring lost self-esteem and for promoting a modern political agenda. Today, hardly anyone argues that the Indians didn't get a raw deal.

This practice of imposing today's attitudes and beliefs on previous generations gave birth to the term "political correctness." It is unfashionable to defend earlier generations of perpetrators and more fashionable to defend earlier generations of victims. Past peoples, whether Indian, white, or any other element of RGE, were products of their own time and place, not ours. Their behavior can be understood and explained only on their terms, not ours. This does not mean they should not be judged by our terms, only that theirs must be explained first.

David McCullough, one of the finest of the modern narrative historians, once told a story that spotlights the issue. The covered-wagon immigrants who crossed the plains in the 1840s and thus started the process that led ultimately to depriving the Indians of their land base and confining them to reservations were the products of the great evangelical movement that swept parts of the East in the 1830s. These white pioneers believed as fervently in their God and his biblical injunctions as the Lakota Sioux believed in Wakantanka and the precepts he laid down for proper behavior. Both groups rendered fealty to their deity through ordained rites and practices. Yet, today we condemn the emigrants for acting in accord with their culture and exonerate the Indians from remaining true to theirs.

This raises the issue of culture in the writing of history. My own pursuit of Sitting Bull brought the challenge into stark relief. I was a product of twentieth-century white, Anglo-Saxon culture taking on a key figure of nineteenth-century Sioux culture. Beyond that, both his culture and mine had changed radically since his life span of 1833–1890. His thoughtworld and mine were poles apart. How to understand and write of the beliefs, attitudes, values, and customs that motivated his actions? From previous works, I already knew a lot about Sioux culture, but I had to learn a lot more.

I did not interview or talk with any modern Sioux. Their culture is almost as distant as mine from the culture of the horse-mounted, buffalo-chasing nomads of Sitting Bull's time. Also, I have found oral tradition passed down through several generations to be of limited use. Tradition changes with each retelling, and details that can be confirmed from the documents are warped or manufactured. What one principally learns is how modern Indians feel about their past.

So I did three things.

First, I studied all the historical and anthropological literature based on interviews with Indians who actually lived the old culture. There is much because at the turn of the century the Smithsonian's Bureau of American Ethnology and some of our great museums sent west dozens of anthropologists, and they gathered the essentials of the old culture before it had been affected by the adaptation of the people to change.

Second, I immersed myself in the papers of Stanley Vestal (Walter S. Campbell), then the author of the standard biography of Sitting Bull, at the University of Oklahoma Library. In the late 1920s and early 1930s he interviewed White Bull and One Bull, Sitting Bull's nephews. They were prime sources because they had lived and ridden with their uncle through most of his life. Vestal recorded his interviews, however, in his own bizarre form of shorthand. Only my knowledge of the subject equipped me to decipher what he had set to paper. These two old Indians, clear-minded and still blessed with sharp memory, provided a host of intimate details critical to understanding Sitting Bull and what he did. I owe Vestal a great debt, not for his flawed biography but for the interviews he left for later scholars to unscramble.

Third, I persuaded the foremost authority on Sioux culture to critique every word I drafted. This was anthropologist Raymond DeMallie at Indiana University. There is nothing in the book that he did not approve. Also, much was deleted of which he did not approve.

The book was highly successful and probably will be remembered as the best of all I wrote. I am indebted to the anthropologists of a century ago, to Stanley Vestal, and to superb anthropologists today.

Another tribute to DeMallie. My first book also required a knowledge of Sioux culture. It was about the Ghost Dance and Wounded Knee, entitled *The Last Days of the Sioux Nation* and published in 1963. In 1982 DeMallie published a critique of dominant scholarship on the Ghost Dance, and he singled me out as exemplar. I did not see the article for several years and then rejected all his criticisms. Since then, however, mainly through my work on Sitting Bull, I came to see that in almost every criticism he was right. My thoughtworld had intruded on the Sioux thoughtworld, attributing to them thought and action seen through my own cultural lenses.

In the spring of 2004 Yale University Press issued a new edition of *Last Days*. I used the new introduction to warn the reader that Ray DeMallie had raised certain objections that I now found valid.

Indian versus white culture is only the clearest of the cultural contrasts a historian confronts in writing on any subject. In virtually every book, I believe, the historian must deal with another culture, be it Indians or soldiers or mountain men or pioneers or outlaws or lawmen. After seven years of work on the Texas Rangers, I am all too aware of how different their culture is from mine. All peoples, regardless of ethnicity, had their subgroups practicing their own distinct brand of the overall culture. True history demands that all these people be treated as products of their own time and place, of their own culture, not ours.

That means that we must always, in writing of the past, immerse ourselves in a culture different from our own.

One final thought. Unlike monographic historians, narrative historians hope to make money. Except for the few giants like David McCullough, H. W. Brands, and Walter Isaacson, one should not think in terms of six figures. Five figures is more realistic, and often a good literary agent is indispensable. I shall always be grateful to Carl D. Brandt, not only for putting me in this league, but for a personal friendship that I treasure. ᘉ

One Writer's Life

Richard S. Wheeler

Richard S. Wheeler was born in 1935, the son of a patent attorney and a former high school English teacher. He attended the University of Wisconsin and embarked upon the first of his careers, journalism, working on newspapers in Phoenix, Oakland, Carson City, and Billings. In midlife, he turned to book editing in the Midwest but left to become a full-time novelist of the West. He is married to Sue Hart, an English professor in Billings, Montana, and divides his time between her home there and his own in Livingston, Montana.

Wheeler is the author of over fifty novels published by Doubleday, M. Evans, Walker and Company, Forge, Bantam, Ballantine, Fawcett, Pinnacle, and New American Library. He is the winner of four Spur Awards, as well as the Owen Wister Award given for lifetime achievement in the literature of the West.

Richard S. Wheeler
(Photo by Kyra Ames)

I am going to write about my life as a novelist. I have never done this before, because I could not imagine why anyone would be interested. But there will be less about me than about the insights I've gained along the way.

In earlier years, I never dreamed I would become a novelist. I had much more important and realistic goals in mind. I wanted to be a fine journalist, edit the opinion page of a large newspaper because I loved the clash of ideas and beliefs, and ultimately become a pundit—a syndicated columnist dispensing wisdom on scores of editorial pages across the country.

Fortunately, I got fired. Not once, but so frequently, from large dailies and small, that it began to dawn on me that newspapering shouldn't be my profession. I got fired for all sorts of reasons—but mostly for incompetence. I was too shy, too introverted to be a good newsman. I wondered whether my serial firings might make me a candidate for the *Guinness Book of Records*. And here's an oddity: At one of the papers at which I was fired, the *Billings Gazette*, I had one of the highest personnel ratings in the newsroom and I was the winner of a major national journalism award, as well as several of the paper's own newsroom awards for the best story of the month.

Which leads you to the obvious conclusion that I am a misfit, and I plead guilty. But being something of an oddball is a valuable trait if you intend to be a novelist. At that time, decades ago, I never dreamed of becoming one. Instead, I became a nonfiction book editor and then a fiction book editor, and both experiences were much more satisfying than daily journalism. A book-length work has substance and there is time to hone and polish it by working with the author. So I learned about book publishing as an editor, something that has served me well in my ultimate career as a novelist.

The great recession of the early 1970s put me out of work. I wasn't fired on that occasion, merely laid off. It turned out to be a fateful hinge in my undistinguished life. There were no jobs. Because of the oil shocks, shortages, the counterculture, and Watergate, the country seemed doomed. After floating fifty or sixty resumes and making bootless applications everywhere in every imaginable field, I retreated to southern Arizona, got a job on a guest ranch wrangling horses and dudes, and began to write westerns. I had always enjoyed recreational fiction such as westerns, and thought maybe I could sell some. And I did. I sold two of them to Jim Menick, Doubleday's western editor, one for one thousand dollars and one for fifteen hundred dollars. I had read everyone from Louis L'Amour to Gordon Shirreffs, and decided maybe I could write one of the things. So, I bravely tackled a novel, not knowing whether I could master the art of fiction. I had a mentor: screenwriter and best-selling novelist Otis Carney. He read my first draft, shook his head, and patiently led me through the fundamentals as we sat on the porch of his Arizona ranch home. I owe my career to him and I have tried ever since to help others as a way of paying back the gift that I received.

It turned out I could write a publishable novel, but only by abandoning much of what I had learned in journalism. I learned how not to *tell* a story, but to *show* it happening, in live scenes. The novelist's closest kin is the playwright, not the newsman. But there were other things that journalism gave me, such as the ability to hustle a story along and the ability to write openings that caught and held a reader. And especially, journalism gave me a sense that I had to convey my material lucidly, logically, transparently, in language that eliminated ambiguity. And I learned to write honestly, without device or flimflam.

So maybe all those things were a benefit.

I wrote those two novels for Doubleday in the 1970s and eventually drifted back to book editing, a field I enjoyed and found satisfying except for the pay scales. They made schoolteachers look rich by comparison. The publishers I worked for happened to be located in the Midwest, in those dreary states that begin with vowels. For a while I edited nonfiction for Open Court Publishing Company in La Salle, Illinois, a scholarly press that specialized in philosophy, science, and mathematics. They had published such people as Albert Einstein and Jean-Paul Sartre, and there I learned my trade. Later, I edited sports books for a publisher in South Bend, Indiana, and edited general nonfiction, mostly public policy, for another house in Illinois. That was satisfying, but I was restless. There had to be more to life than flat prairies, cornfields, and uninspiring small towns.

In 1982 I took a momentous step, joined the Western Writers of America and attended the group's convention in Santa Fe, New Mexico. I didn't know a soul and wandered about shyly, blotting it all up, and discovering how much I loved these people and the literary life. I met dozens of writers who are now my closest friends and literary colleagues.

One afternoon I sat down at a table in the patio at the Inn of Loretto and introduced myself to the strangers there, one of whom was Sara Ann Freed, then editor for Walker and Company. I had a novel called *Winter Grass* to sell, but I had the good sense not to hawk it in purely social circumstances. We simply talked, and I enjoyed her and her husband and absorbed every word they said about New York literary life. Later, I wrote her and asked her if she would look at a western I had written. She did, and she bought it, and it was duly published by Walker and became a Spur Award finalist. But I did not abandon book editing. A twenty-five hundred dollar advance for a novel wasn't going to support me for long.

Sara Ann Freed moved on to M. Evans, and then went over to Mysterious Press, where she became a senior editor and vice president of Time Warner Books and a celebrated New York editor before her untimely death. But before then, when she was at M. Evans, she bought five more of my novels, standing beside me through my apprenticeship period and seeing in me more than I saw in myself.

In 1985 opportunity came to me. I had always loved the West and itched to return there, but lacked the means. When the western editor at Walker resigned, I saw my chance and wrote the late Sam Walker to inquire whether I could edit his western line from Montana. I had, by then, some experience as a fiction book editor and had published three novels of my own. The answer was yes. I would get one thousand dollars a book to acquire and edit Walker's westerns, which were being published at the rate of one a month. So, I fled the flatlands of the Midwest, never so happy to escape a dead-end life, and set up shop in the A-frame log home of an old newspaper friend near Lincoln, Montana. Little did I know that just a few miles away there lived a man in a crude shack whose obsession was bombing anyone he believed to be the harbinger of technological change. Of the Unabomber I knew nothing, but there, in the wilderness, I had my chance: an inexpensive place to live in Montana's glorious wilds, a small editing income, and the freedom to write my heart out. Those were wondrous times. I slaved away summer and winter, selecting and editing manuscripts, and writing novels. But it was as an acquiring editor that I made some difference to my field. I published several first novels, among them one by Gary Svee, who went on to win a Spur Award some years later. I published the first novel of Sam Brown, who is, I believe, one of the best of the traditional western novelists. I started Lenore Carroll of Kansas City. I put several other careers on track.

Selecting manuscripts for publication is a task fraught with joy and pain. A company's profits and prestige ride on your decisions. Your discernment is on the line. Like most people, I had often wondered how some worthless novel or other ever got into print—and now the shoe was on the other foot, and I knew people out there would be wondering how my selections ever made it into print.

One of the most painful burdens borne by an acquiring editor is saying no to friends. I never found a very good way to do it. I had met numerous authors at writers' conventions and many of them wanted me to purchase their novels. They were colleagues in a field of literature we all loved. By far the most preferable course in such circumstances was utter candor: the novel simply failed for one reason or another or didn't fit the line. But some people take such news angrily. I received several bitter letters. I wasn't the rankest of cowards but neither was I very courageous when it came to rejecting stories that weren't up to my standards. Fortunately, Walker had an in-house editor, the gifted Jackie Johnson, and we formed ourselves into an editorial committee and decided that each story we bought should pass muster with both of us. Later, after I left Walker, she continued as the company's western editor and successfully advanced the line. There are, of course, intermediate options between acceptance and rejection, such as telling the author to revise their work, based on the notes I provided, and then resubmit. I was able to salvage a few troubled stories that way.

One of those I helped in that fashion was the late Fred Bean. I sent him two or three pages of densely typed notes on a novel that just missed. He told me that I was the first editor that had ever taken the time to give him any advice and that the notes gave him the keys to publication. At any rate, armed with my critique and his own great skill, he went on to achieve success and became a Spur Award finalist. I was also able to help Mike and Kathy Gear get launched. They sent me a whole box-load of lengthy western manuscripts, all much too long for the Walker line, but over time I read each of them, sent critiques, and that intelligent couple made good use of them and launched great careers. That was the first editorial criticism they ever received. Later, I helped Kathy Gear analyze an unmarketable story, which she promptly turned into one she could and did sell. I offered some advice, but it was their own determination, industry, willingness to deal with criticism, and knowledge of their subject that shaped their successful careers.

One of the novels I bought for Walker was oversized and I had to get permission from the company to buy it. It had some remarkably good storytelling in it, and the author knew his field. But it was the author's first novel and was flawed in various ways that I was pretty confident could be repaired with a little editorial direction. The story was good enough that I thought it might win a first-novel award if its problems were corrected. So I spent an unusual amount of time analyzing it, taking notes, and then sending the notes to the author with the suggestion that he deal with the weaknesses.

Much to my dismay, he rejected all my suggestions. Not only that, he largely rejected my routine line editing, stetting much of what I had done, even when I was correcting grammar or clarifying a muddy sentence. At that point I left Walker and the novel became Jackie Johnson's problem. Soon thereafter, I received a copy of an extraordinary letter in which several Walker editors, each of whom had read all or part of the novel, begged the author to implement my suggestions. In all my years of publishing, I've never seen or heard of anything like that. It was amazing: the company felt that the novel had great potential, and several of its editors wrote the author, pleading for the changes that would eliminate its flaws. But the author remained as rigid in the face of three or four editors as he had with me, and so, sadly, a potentially fine novel went into print with flaws.

I was saddened. Years later, that author asked me to blurb another novel, which I gladly did. I sent him a strong blurb, but in my cover letter to him, I noted that one of the story lines fell apart at the end because he left a character in a jam and facing death, gave no hint of how the character got out of it, and then produced the character unscathed at the end of the novel. Well, the author used my blurb, but not my advice!

Let me point out here that professional etiquette is involved in something like this. Although the request for the blurb came from the editor, I wrote the author privately about the problem in the story. I did not write the editor. It is not proper for an author to insert himself between another author and his editor, or between the author and the publisher. Don't meddle. Treat other authors as you would hope to be treated.

In 1986 I signed a three-book contract with Tor that marked the beginning of a change in my life and work. I had proposed a series called Skye's West to Tor's executive editor, Michael Seidman. It would feature a former mountain man who had become a wilderness guide, and who had two wives, one Crow, the other Shoshone. Up until then I had written ordinary horse opera. Now, in a larger format,

I had the chance to grow, to write something richer. Up until then, my horizons had been limited. Write entertainment, make a buck, fill the stories with action and conflict, keep readers riveted, and pocket the royalties. Now, suddenly, I yearned for more. I began to reflect on what fiction is really about. Should fiction merely tell stories? Might a function of fiction also be to pierce to the truth of the human condition? Could a story instruct a reader, or present ideals or values worth honoring? Could I make a story *more* entertaining by making it richer? Could I begin to write more seriously in a field notorious for rigidity? Could I begin to break loose from the old stereotypes and write something new?

I decided I could. Barnaby Skye, my hero, was anything but a traditional western protagonist. He was a refugee from the Royal Navy. I gave him a tender side, a gentleness toward others and toward animals. I let him reflect on the nature of good and evil. I discovered, as I developed him, that remnants of his old Anglican faith remained and guided his conduct. I let him probe into the difficulties of cross-cultural marriage and intimacy. I introduced something one doesn't see in traditional western heroes: a sense of shame, and a feeling of helplessness now and then when he confronts something that overwhelms him. I made him a binge drinker. Was I turning him into some sensitive modern? Of course not. I kept him true to his mid-nineteenth-century times. But he certainly was not the typical Gary Cooper-type hero.

The series did well, and with each novel I expanded Skye's character, taking him farther and farther from the rigid forms of the traditional western story. And this, in turn, evoked a thirst in me to write more meaningful literature. Ever since then I've wrestled with the gods of literature, and my ideas of what constitutes a good novel are still evolving. I have reached the point now where my goal is to write for the ages and not simply for today's market. I believe there are universal truths, recognized by each generation, that can be explicated in a novel, and that if I depict these truths well, my novels will be as fresh and meaningful to future generations, which may be radically different from ours in other ways.

But don't construe any of this to mean that I've abandoned storytelling. Spinning a gripping story is the bedrock of fiction, and if you fail, and if the reader gets bored and puts the book down, you've lost. If you bore readers, you are not a good novelist, no matter how profound you might be. For some reason this humble reality eludes critics, which is why they so often celebrate dull and unreadable books.

My efforts to grow into a novelist ran into setbacks. One of these was Epstein-Barr disease, which sapped my strength for two years in the early nineties. During that period I wrote a series for Pinnacle called the Rocky Mountain Company, which had great potential because it was based on rich material no other novelist had touched—the buffalo robe trade. Each day I forced myself to get up and write for an hour or two in spite of a low fever and indescribable weariness. I still had to make a living, no matter how sick I felt or depressed I was about a disease that has no cure and can persist for years before burning itself out. As you might expect, these books were not my best work, though I wrestled with them all the harder, knowing that my physical condition was affecting my work. But when I look back upon that period, I do so with pride: I wrote the best books I could, and kept on writing. And that series was recently reprinted, very successfully.

The marketplace has a way of imprisoning an author in pigeonholes, and even today I find my big historical novels in the western bays when they should be on the general fiction shelves. It is one of those burdens an author must bear. I have no way of telling thousands of booksellers around the country that some of what I'm writing now has utterly nothing to do with Max Brand or Zane Grey or Louis L'Amour, and is not genre fiction. The late Graham Greene made a useful distinction: he said he wrote "entertainments" and he wrote "novels." He meant that some of his shorter and lighter works were intended to entertain, while his more serious works—what he called his novels—explored the human condition. In his day, the distinction worked well. Booksellers had no trouble sorting out his mysteries and adventure stories from his more serious work and shelving them accordingly. Today that would no longer work well because of the mindlessness of the book distribution system. A writer who begins by producing genre fiction is doomed to be regarded as a genre novelist no matter what he writes, which is something that chafes and grates on my soul, and which I try fecklessly to transcend.

I spent those middle years of my writing life pondering the very nature and purpose of fiction. But I was also determined to master every known technique of storytelling and voice so that I might have the craft and cunning to captivate my readers. Beginnings are very important. You win or lose a reader in the first few pages. In journalism, you focus on the lead, the opening sentences, which either captures or loses your readers. In fiction you have a few paragraphs to do it. The proper technique, of course, is to plunge immediately into a dilemma, and then feed the backstory into the ongoing present story. If you spend too long explaining who the character is and what the circumstances are, you have a static beginning and lose your reader.

The best way I know of to start a story is to use a simple formula: "The trouble began when . . ." That one is foolproof. Begin with the trouble. I have often employed that formula to begin a story. Here is how I started a recent Skye novel:

It never occurred to Barnaby Skye that domestic discord could ruin a rendezvous or even threaten his future as a mountaineer. Even less had he imagined that it would transform his life. But his young Crow wife, Victoria, was unhappy and on the brink of leaving him, and that was how the trouble began.

One of the things authors worry about is the passive verb, especially the various forms of the verb *is*, which expresses nothing more than a state of being. I myself have critiqued many a manuscript by circling the *wases* on every page as a reminder to employ livelier verbs. Usually a verb can be found that eliminates the various forms of *is*, and it is possible to juggle sentences in ways that make the passive verb unnecessary. In most of my work, until recently, I made an enormous effort to get rid of passive verbs, often rejiggering sentences until they scarcely resembled the originals. But then I began asking myself what is wrong with using *was*. Surely it expresses a valid meaning—that something existed. Maybe that was just what I wanted to say: that something existed. Yes, it is a verb to be avoided. If you write, "The cliff loomed ahead," that is certainly better than saying, "The cliff was ahead." Avoid *was* if you can.

But doubts kept nagging me, and out of curiosity I finally turned to the writings of the novelist most celebrated for voice and style, Ernest Hemingway. I surveyed portions of several novels, and the result astonished me. He used *was* frequently, and I came across passages in which *was* appeared promiscuously. Was Hemingway simply sloppy? No, he knew exactly what he was doing, and he didn't much care whether his verb forms were passive. Story is what counts. If the story is riveting, that's all that matters. Yes, sometimes a good verb helps the story, but conversely, you can distract your readers with a showy display of exotic verbs, and suddenly your reader is not lost in the story, but busy absorbing your prose style, and you are being a beauty queen instead of a novelist. The choice is yours. If you wish to be a gaudy writer, placing style above substance, with your voice boiling out of every sentence, go for the fancy verb. But *was* has the value of being invisible, and that in itself has merit.

The same is true of attribution. In my earlier novels I avoided "he said" or "she said" as much as possible, and used all sorts of utterance verbs that now embarrass me: snarled, laughed, joked, snickered, spat, heckled, yawned. I no longer employ any of them, and can barely stand to read the early stories in which I employed them promiscuously. That simple attribution, *said*, is invisible to readers and doesn't jar them, which is good. It simply identifies the speaker of the dialogueue, and I rarely use any other attribution now.

My approach to telling a story these days is simpler. The important thing, as far as I can see, is utter transparency. I've abandoned most of the artifices and skills I had learned in favor of plain and unadorned prose that is not calculated to express my "voice," whatever that is, or achieve any effect or impact on my reader. All these artifices may be valid, and it's up to you to decide whether to employ them or not. But no technique, skill, protocol, or artifice is half so important as telling a great story. I have no voice, if voice is defined as structural artifice. I do have a voice, if voice is defined as a body of beliefs, attitudes, feelings, passions, and a sense of the sacred, which appears in novel after novel of mine. If I have a voice, it rises from substance, not style. And that is how I want it. I certainly don't want my works remembered for their mascara.

I have come to admire copy editors. They are practitioners of an arcane art that is beyond me. They are the temple priests of literature, imbued with occult knowledge they don't share with mere mortals. When I write *which*, they change it to *that*; when I write *that*, they change it to *which*. When I write *further,* they change it to *farther;* when I write *farther,* they change it to *further.* The spellings in my dictionaries offend them, and I know not what authorities they use to trump my authorities. But they rescue me from great embarrassments, and I always rejoice when a good copy editor has been assigned to my novel. The copy editors possess the keys to the kingdom, and my counsel to other authors is to let the copy editors perform their sacred rites over your novel. Take heed, and resist them rarely. Once in a long while they practice ritual sacrifice, murdering your novel on the high altar of the gods, in which case pronounce the magic and holy word, *stet*, and all will be well.

Early in my writing life, I supposed that conflict was essential in storytelling. Without conflict, you had no story. Conflict was largely defined as people or groups at cross purposes with each other, but it also included struggles against nature or machinery or anything else. Thus, Hemingway's celebrated novel *The Old Man and the Sea* pitted a man against his own faltering body, brutal heat and dehydration, the sea itself, as well as a great fish. But in recent years I've found the idea of conflict to be inadequate and constricting. There's more to literature than conflict. I can write a fine, gripping story with no conflict in it, at least as most authors define conflict. I prefer a different word and a larger concept. Fiction is about *dilemma*. The protagonist simply faces a dilemma of some sort, often without visible conflict. Maybe a young man graduating from high school faces the dilemma of choosing a career or vocation. Maybe a woman who has every material thing the world can offer is tempted to surrender it all and become a nun. Values are her dilemma. I've concluded that dilemma is a much broader and richer perception than conflict. To be sure, one can stretch the idea of conflict to include dilemma, but I find myself writing truer and deeper when I consider my characters' dilemma.

Over the years, I've endured a great deal of criticism and dished some out. That seems to be the fate of authors. I've received bad reviews and good, and remember the bad ones longer than I remember the glowing ones. There also is implicit criticism in the editing and copyediting process, and even in proofreading. Dealing with criticism is a major occupation for all novelists. We join writing groups, whose very purpose is to criticize, and there is obvious value in that. Criticism helps us see our work through others eyes, and helps overcome our own blindness. When we go to workshops, we know our writing is going to be criticized, and we hope to profit from it. We secretly wish to receive only praise, but we all know better than that. Praise may massage our vanity, but it usually won't help us write better. I have always found criticism to be wounding and painful, and I imagine it is because I am thin-skinned.

The standard advice given to writers is that criticism of our work is not the same as criticism of our selves, and we must learn to separate the two. The idea is that when someone is finding fault with something I've written, it doesn't mean the critic is attacking me. I've tried hard to believe that, and have solemnly intoned that bit of wisdom to numerous students in workshops. The problem is, it just ain't so.

If you are like me, you have pulled your writing straight out of your soul and mind and heart. I write about my innermost feelings, dreams, dreads, visions, sacred beliefs, and inadvertently I write about my various kinks, weaknesses, follies, stupidities, and embarrassing secrets. I cannot for the life of me separate my writing from myself, and the harsh truth is that any criticism of my novels is criticism of me, and there is absolutely no escaping it. When someone doesn't like aspects of my stories, he doesn't like aspects of me. My soul and my work are much too intimately tied for me to pretend that I'm not being criticized when my work is under fire.

But out of this understanding comes strength. Yes, I'm being criticized, and yes, I can use what I learn not only to improve my stories, but to improve *me*, or at least grasp how I give offense, or fail to meet expectations. Is my story boring? Then, I'm boring. Are my characters clichés? Then I'm superficial. So, if you are like me, your only recourse is to grasp the nettle. My work *is* me. The miracle in all this is that literary criticism is a form of therapy, of psychoanalysis, by which I am steadily growing as both a writer and a person. One of the things I've come to grips with is that readers know a great deal about me, including many traits I routinely hid from the world. My readers know my every failing—but they also know my strengths and whatever is admirable in me, because these things also show up in my characters.

But I sure prefer a rave review!

I am indebted to my friend Win Blevins for the following idea, but it is one I subscribe to so strongly that I have made it my own. A few years ago, Win wrestled in print with the widespread notion that a novelist cannot write insightfully and accurately about other sorts of people. That is, a male novelist cannot adequately depict a woman or grasp what it means to be a woman; a white novelist cannot begin to fathom what it must be like to live as a black, and suffer life as blacks suffer it, and so on. This notion lies at the heart of much contemporary literary thinking, especially feminist and multicultural criticism, and is responsible for the effort to wean English curricula from the study of "dead white males."

The idea appalled Win Blevins and it appalled me. Is it really true that I cannot, because I am male, write about women or depict women accurately? The flaw in this proposition is that it denies our common humanity, our intelligence, our imagination, and our empathy. Simply by virtue of the fact that we are human beings in intimate contact, men have an excellent idea of how it must be to live a woman's life, and vice versa. We understand how our differing bodies govern and limit our conduct. We communicate. Women tell us how life is, and we males tell women how life is. We have intelligence with which to process what we learn. We do research, asking specific questions to fill in the blanks. The notion that I can't write about people who are different from myself is preposterous and a libel on the whole human race, not just me. It assumes we are too dumb, too obtuse, too insensitive to grasp the nature of any life other than our own. I am here to tell you that as you evolve your skills, you will depict the opposite sex, and people of various races and cultures, with exquisite sensitivity and truthfulness, and if you believe it can't be done, then you believe that humans are subhuman.

I will, however, offer one small caveat. When I was a book editor, I discovered that female authors depicted male characters much better than male authors depicted female characters. I don't know why. I've checked my observation with other editors, and found that they have noted the same thing. For whatever reason, women are the better students of the opposite sex. I leave it to the sociologists to explain why.

The writer's life is filled with highs and lows. We are lifted by good reviews, depressed by bad sales numbers. We feel good when we move a few books at a signing, bad when we're skunked and walk out of the store without selling one book. We wait anxiously for news about our proposals and contracts, chafe when the royalty statements and checks are late, sweat out deadlines, rejoice when we learn there has been a subsidiary rights sale.

One of the great moments in my writing life arrived some years ago, when I came home after a day out, and discovered a fax dangling from my machine with a string of exclamation points on it. But before I tell you what all those points were exclaiming about, let me step back a bit. One of my early novels was a traditional western called *Where the River Runs*. I had wanted to call it *Follow the River*, but James Thom had gotten there ahead of me. It was a story of a young woman whose fiancé, a captain, had vanished in the wilderness while on a treaty-nego-tiating mission. She goes after him, and the novel is essentially a love story. M. Evans published it, and later, a South Korean publisher picked it up, paying a modest two thousand dollars for it against a 6 percent royalty. However, by the time the two agents and the South Korean gov-ernment took their share, the total came to less than fourteen hundred dollars. Found money. Fine. I forgot about it. Later there arrived some copies of the Korean trade paper edition, which of course I could not read. Meanwhile it had gone into a Tor mass-market edition here in the United States. And then one fine April day, the fax arrived from my agent, Barbara Puechner. A check drafted on a Korean export-import bank had arrived to the tune of $35,000, and that amount was the net after the Korean agent and government had taken their cut. My agent took out her cut, and sent me the balance, which came to roughly $30,000. The novel had become a best-seller there, selling about 125,000 copies. Later, more checks came, and the novel finally yielded close to $50,000, the most I've ever gotten for a book.

In Korea there is no returns system, by which sellers can send back to the publisher the books they don't sell and get full credit for the returned book. So I received the full amount of my royalties at once, and nothing was held as a reserve against returns, as is the case in this country. I regard the returns system to be the most pernicious and uneconomic arrangement in American business. It forces publishers to print many more copies than they ever sell, which raises the prices of books, and it forces authors to wait for years to get their entire earned royalties from their publishers, which hold back some of the earnings in case they are deluged with returned copies of the title. The return shipping and accounting all add to the inefficiency, further jacking up the price of books and eroding the profit not only of publishers and authors, but the booksellers as well.

At any rate, that serendipitous bonanza was one of my great moments and a milestone in my writer's life. There are painful moments, too. I'll describe one that still haunts me. Some years ago I switched to a new agent because my former one was cutting back the clients in her firm. My new agent was one of the most powerful in New York, with best-seller clients and plenty of clout. I had known him for years, and we were friends—and still are friends. He negotiated a contract for a California gold rush novel I wanted to do. I did the research, and from it I shaped my story. I wanted to include several elements: the over-land rush to California in 1849; the rush via the fever-ridden Panama route; the gold rush widows, as they were called—left behind by their husbands; and the tragic fate of the Californios, the Mexican people of California who were dispossessed by the gold rush. I also intended to turn all this into a powerful and moving love story.

And thus I began writing. When I was eighty or ninety pages into it, my new agent asked to critique what I was doing. I complied reluctantly, because I don't like to show my work until I am ready, and beginnings are especially subject to change as the story develops. But I sent him my work and in due course received a devastating letter. He didn't like my characters, didn't like the story line, and suggested I ditch everything and build the story around a minor character, a tinhorn gambler.

That stunned me. Here was one of the most powerful men in pub-lishing telling me to forget everything and make the novel about a gambler. Forget the research, forget my love story, forget the Panama passage, forget the Californios. Forget my dream and the novel gestating within me. I fell into agony, not knowing what to do. This was the lowest point in my entire writing life. But during that midnight of the soul, I took stock of myself, my skills, my objective, my dreams—and decided I was going to continue with the story I had started even though I was, in essence, rejecting the views of one of the shrewdest and most successful men in publishing. I *had* to or surrender my literary life. It had come down to that. If I had surrendered, the heart would have gone out of me and out of my novels and I would now be doing something else.

The result was my novel *Sierra*. It was indeed flawed, and my editor sent me pages of notes suggesting changes, which I incorporated. I had written the novel that was in me and it was eventually published, receiving the best reviews I have ever gotten, and then it won the Spur Award for Best Novel of the West for 1996. It earned a substantial amount of money, twice its advance.

Somehow or other, I had found the courage to stay with my vision. I learned something: I will never again show my work in progress until I am ready to show it. Now, you will note the moral of this episode—defend your literary integrity—is exactly the opposite of the moral of the earlier episode I described to you when I, as an editor, grieved the rigidity of the author of a first novel who would change nothing. Am I offering contradictory advice here? Am I seeing one episode from the eyes of an editor and the other through the eyes of an author?

No, there is no contradiction. The rigid author, writing his first novel, lacked the seasoning to see the problems that several Walker and Company editors begged him to correct. But at the time I wrote *Sierra*, I had many books behind me, knew my strengths and limitations, and knew the richness of my research. There are no hard and fast rules. There are times when an author is wise to heed advice and listen. There are seasons when an author must have the courage of his convictions and reject well-meaning advice that would gravely damage his work.

Virtually all authors wrestle, to some extent, with their publishers. The very nature of the relationship between author, editor, and publisher generates problems. Most are resolved amiably by adult people. I have been very fortunate to have, as my publishers for many years, some of the kindest and most gracious people in the publishing world. My publisher, Forge, is run by Tom Dougherty, who goes out of his way to make life pleasant for his authors. One of the things he does is to permit authors to check on all sales figures at any time. I can call and find out how many copies of a book were shipped, what the returns look like, what the net sales look like. This makes authors partners in the business. But for some inexplicable reason many publishers hide such information from authors, treating them essentially as the enemy, operating on the presumption that the less an author knows, the better.

One of Tom Dougherty Associates' many virtues is its willingness to consult with authors about covers and jackets. The company usually asks me whether I have any jacket or cover ideas. This courtesy is rare among publishers. The standard reason for excluding authors from the process of developing the book packaging is that authors are not competent to contribute anything, and are sometimes kooky. Covers are, after all, pure advertising which is a concept that eludes authors. When I was a book editor I heard all the old stories about authors who insisted on something bizarre on their jackets, and in truth such things do crop up now and then. But Forge and Tor are aware of the reverse side of that equation: the author may have a valuable idea about how to market a book. This is especially true in my field, the early American West, where I have expertise not readily at hand in New York. Recently my publishers asked me about my preference for one of my Skye's West books, which is set largely in a Crow Indian village. I replied that a turn-of-the-century artist, Joseph Sharp, spent years painting the village life of the Crows. All this resulted in the development of a gorgeous cover built around a Sharp painting of a Crow village.

But such accommodations sometimes backfire. I was asked to suggest cover ideas for my first two frontier mining town books, *Cashbox* and *Goldfield*, and I did, proposing that the cover art depict the faces of the characters, against a mining town background. The books were packaged in just that fashion—and did poorly. The covers made the books seem lightweight, soap opera stuff. Much chastened by the result, I withdrew from the process of influencing my own covers. In other words, I learned to trust the expertise of the packagers and designers. They were, after all, the experts. My hard-won humility paid off: left alone, the designers came up with the finest and most elegant covers I have ever enjoyed. These new cover designs create a thematic image of literary excellence for my books that was superior to my wildest imaginings, and I am in debt to the book packagers at Forge for giving me dream jackets.

A book is a small enterprise. Publishers do not enjoy mass production and cannot advertise a single mass-produced product like Wheaties or Ford pickup trucks. Every item in a publisher's line is custom made, presents its own opportunities, problems, and limitations, and must be sold on its own terms. There is little money for promotion in the budget of a typical book, and such promotion money is expended on cataloguing the book and selling it to the company's own reps, who then fan out and sell it to wholesalers and retailers. Given the deep silence in which most books are launched, it is a miracle that any sell. But there is no help for it. Generally, publishers who sink huge sums into advertising a title don't see much in return. The money is simply lost.

This leads to considerable contention between publishers and authors, and I often hear bitter authors complaining about the inattention their title received. I have done such complaining myself. To make matters even more painful, when a book doesn't do well, the author is blamed—never the publisher, no matter how badly the book was packaged and marketed. Even if the cover is abysmal, or the jacket copy turgid, even if it is sold to the wrong markets, or mislabeled on the spine, the author is blamed if the book fails, and when contract time rolls around, those poor sales are held against the author. In all my years of writing for several publishers, I have never had a publisher or anyone in a publishing house say to me, "That was a lousy cover, and the low sales weren't your fault." It just isn't done.

Sometimes the best of intentions turn out badly. Here is a painful story, but one without blame. Circumstance alone is responsible for what happened. Several years ago, my editor, Harriet McDougal, told me that she and my publisher, Tom Dougherty, wanted me to do a city novel—that is, for me to set my story in a large western city that was a good book town. The reason, she explained, was that my sales numbers were down, and it would be possible to rebuild them by concentrating the entire publicity budget upon a small geographic area instead of spreading it thinly across the country. She said when the book was published there would be a media blitz to create a "circus effect" that would generate such intense publicity that the book would actually sell better than with national publicity.

That was fine, and we chose Denver, a big city with an established book-buying population. I wrote one of my best novels, *Second Lives*, which was set in Denver's Gilded Age and included some of Denver's early citizens. Publication day arrived, and the book received excellent book trade reviews—not one negative word from any of them. But meanwhile, things had changed. Harriet had cut back her editing and transferred me to another editor. The publicity staff had turned over, and the new people knew nothing about the plan. I was aware of this, so in advance of publication I told them that I had written this novel expressly at the request of my editor and publisher to be the focus of a Denver blitz.

Well, I guess they didn't get the message. They did send me out with my friend and colleague Norman Zollinger. But all the planning intended to boost my numbers didn't happen. They set up no book signings in Denver, though we did go to Fort Collins and two other small Colorado towns. There were no local reviews, no ads in the papers, radio, or television, no print or electronic interviews, no razzmatazz. When Norman and I walked into the Tattered Cover, Denver's great bookstore, we discovered that the saleswoman in charge of fiction did not know that *Second Lives* was set in Denver. No one from Forge had called to tell them. So much for any circus effect. In essence, the book died that week. It had been written especially for Denver sales and when the publicity didn't materialize, it was a goner.

These things happen. The best thing to do is to laugh and forget your troubles.

Well, what of the author during all these years. Did I grow? Am I reaching new readers? Have my goals changed? Yes, to all. Remember, I was the guy who backed into fiction with no more in mind than making a buck. Now I'm at the other end of the spectrum. I want to write fiction that not only entertains, but endures from generation to generation, that touches upon universal truths, that explores the human condition and helps people understand life, that inspires people in their daily lives, and much more. When I examine myself realistically, I'm pretty sure I won't even come close to any of this. But that is what my voyage amounts to now as I near the sunset of my life.

When you aspire to great things, you assume great burdens. One of these is independence of mind. It is amazing how few people in this world study all sides of great issues and draw their own conclusions regardless of whatever is trendy or current at the time. The Germans have a good word, *Zeitgeist*, which means the spirit of the times. I don't really know how Zeitgeist works, but I do know that some things are in and other things are out. Some things will endure, and some will not. History has a way of winnowing out nonsense. It is more important for the independent-minded to weigh these issues on their merits. A novelist hoping to command a promontory or write something that will last longer than the ever-changing trends of the times needs to take a longer and deeper view of the progress of the human race. The author who dissents from the trendiness of the times is at risk of writing books that don't sell well. If the author is courageous, he or she will write what lies within no matter what the world thinks of it.

The other qualities required of an author are reverence and love and a yearning for truth. If you cannot marvel at an ant, you cannot write worthwhile literature. If you do not love, your work will be mean and small. If you cannot reverence the accumulated wisdom and genius of our forebears, you are doomed to write trivia. If you cannot love your spouses, fathers and mothers, sisters and brothers, sons and daughters, friends and strangers, who wrestle with the awesome burden of living life well, then you haven't taken the first step toward understanding. If you do not seek truth in the midst of the world's complexity and ambiguity, then you will lack honesty.

We live in a period without great novels largely because our most prominent novelists are merely trendy, and publishers encourage trendiness because it improves profits. Given the state of American publishing, with its emphasis on instant gratification of reader, editor, and shareholder, I doubt that a truly great novel could even be published today.

I am discovering that the author of a novel that is not trendy, or politically correct, pays a price. A few years ago I published my first contemporary novel, *The Buffalo Commons*, which deals with land-use issues in the modern West and pits environmentalists against a ranching family. I carefully presented all sides but that is not what politically correct readers want. The novel was launched without support from my publisher. Nicolas Evans subsequently published *The Loop*, which covered the same ground, but he chose to make his story politically correct: in his novel ranchers were evil, wildlife biologists were good. His book remained high on the best-seller charts for weeks. Mine didn't sell well. But I am proud of my novel. It is honest. It depicted the strengths and weaknesses in each side. It delved into the reasons we are set upon this earth. But I especially cherish it because it was not trendy.

I have no illusions about my abilities. My novels fall into oblivion a few years after they are written. But that doesn't mean I shouldn't try, or shouldn't dream. Even an obscure, second-rate novelist can leave behind him one chapter, one page, or one paragraph that is immortal because it strikes a truth. Let me leave behind one bright shining page.

I have received a great gift. I came to the writer's life late in my days, but it turned out to be the vocation I was born for, the reason I was set upon this earth. There have been heartaches, but the joys far out-number and overwhelm them. I have been blessed with fine publishers and editors and literary colleagues, but I have also been blessed with enthusiastic readers, many of whom have become my friends. Even if my numbers fail and I can sell no more books, I will keep on writing. I am going to reach for the impossible dream during the last years of my life. ∪